Talking Stick

"*Talking Stick* is written with all of the clarity and intelligence we expect from Steve's work, but this book is enlivened by the profound passion of his heart. As such, this is one of those rare books that becomes a teacher. While passing the talking stick is familiar protocol in shamanic circles, the art and warriorship of becoming a peacemaker is not. Today's shamanic practitioners are being called out by the illness of our time to embody their practices, heart and soul. Here is a teacher who shows us how to step from being contemporary people using shamanic skills to being shamanic people living in the contemporary world and becoming the medicine needed by our time."

CHRISTINA LEE PRATT, FOUNDER AND DIRECTOR OF THE LAST MASK CENTER, TEACHER, HEALER, AND AUTHOR OF *AN ENCYCLOPEDIA OF SHAMANISM*

Steve offers us a teaching central to our needs as a people. He guides us in a practice of peace, not only as avoidance of violence but as realization of our true nature. At the heart of this approach is *listening*, a core value of powerfully transformational poetry and music as well. *Talking Stick* is about healing the world."

GEORGE QUASHA, POET AND ARTIST AND AUTHOR OF *AXIAL STONES: AN ART OF PRECARIOUS BALANCE*

"Steve Beyer has taken a bold step toward illuminating a path to conflict transformation through a process of peacemaking by which people meet eye to eye, listen, and speak with an open heart. In this way, sacred spaces are created and relationships are affirmed. *Talking Stick* is a primer for all those seeking supportive change, be it in the therapy office or in the wilderness."

DENE BERMAN, PH.D., CLINICAL PSYCHOLOGIST AND COAUTHOR OF *THE PROMISE OF WILDERNESS THERAPY* AND *THE BACKCOUNTRY CLASSROOM*

". . . a delightful and inspiring book. . . . a unique and valuable how-to guide, chock full of practices mixed in with insights and challenges. In embarking on the spiritual journey, the reader will sense this wise elder's presence—an unexpected and special pleasure."

DOUGLAS THOMSON, PH.D., PROFESSOR OF CRIMINAL JUSTICE AND SOCIOLOGY AT CHICAGO STATE UNIVERSITY AND FOUNDER OF JUSTICE NOT PRISONS

"Beyer's gentle and easy style offers a wealth of traditional wisdom about peacemaking, human relationships, and human nature. Don't be fooled by his good-natured and humane voice. Beneath his words lies a warm sophistication that comes from great experience."

ALLAN COMBS, PH.D., COEDITOR OF *THOMAS BERRY, DREAMER OF THE EARTH*

"*Talking Stick* is a strong reference for understanding how conflict can be transformed in home, school, and community environments. When everyone is heard, there is a calm that allows for collaboration and consensus. *Talking Stick* provides another way of thinking about how our world can become a more peaceful place."

PATRICIA YONKA, MEMBER OF THE AMERICAN MONTESSORI SOCIETY PEACE COMMITTEE, MONTESSORI REPRESENTATIVE TO THE UNITED NATIONS, AND FOUNDING BOARD MEMBER AND FACILITATOR OF THE GLOBAL CITIZENSHIP ACTION PROJECT

Talking Stick

PEACEMAKING AS
A SPIRITUAL PATH

STEPHAN V. BEYER

Bear & Company
Rochester, Vermont • Toronto, Canada

Bear & Company
One Park Street
Rochester, Vermont 05767
www.BearandCompanyBooks.com

Bear & Company is a division of Inner Traditions International

Library of Congress Cataloging-in-Publication Data
Names: Beyer, Stephan V., 1943– author.
Title: Talking stick : peacemaking as a spiritual path / Stephan V. Beyer.
Description: Rochester : Bear & Company, 2016. | Includes index.
Identifiers: LCCN 2015047027 (print) | LCCN 2016006527 (e-book) |
    ISBN 9781591432579 (paperback) | ISBN 9781591432586 (e-book)
Subjects: LCSH: Conflict management. | Reconciliation. |
    BISAC: FAMILY & RELATIONSHIPS / Conflict Resolution. |
    BODY, MIND & SPIRIT / Inspiration & Personal Growth. |
    PSYCHOLOGY / Interpersonal Relations.
Classification: LCC HM1126 .B49 2016 (print) | LCC HM1126 (e-book)
    DDC 303.6/9—dc23
LC record available at http://lccn.loc.gov/2015047027

Printed and bound in the United States by Versa Press, Inc.

10 9 8 7 6 5 4 3 2 1

Text design and layout by Virginia Scott Bowman
This book was typeset in Garamond Premier Pro with Folks, Rage Italic, and Avenir used as display typefaces

To send correspondence to the author of this book, mail a first-class letter to the author c/o Inner Traditions • Bear & Company, One Park Street, Rochester, VT 05767, and we will forward the communication.

Contents

PART III
Walking the Peace Path

Acknowledgments

This book is the result of inspiration, advice, and encouragement by many companions on the peacemaking path. I dedicate this book in grateful thanks—

To Tomas Ramirez, road chief, true circlekeeper, warrior of the heart, my older brother on the path.

To Sparrow Hart, my friend and teacher, for our times together in the wilderness, and for our night-long discussions of ceremony, the heroic journey, and the yearnings of the soul.

To Doug Thomson, for encouraging me to teach in the Department of Criminal Justice at Chicago State University, and for our long talks on the nature of justice in society, and to the students in my CSU courses and seminars on restorative justice and nonviolent resistance, who taught me, I am sure, much more than I taught them.

To Peter Newman, for many years the heart of restorative justice in Chicago and the Cook County juvenile justice system, and to Elizabeth Vastine, for many years head of the Neighborhood Restorative Justice Institute, who both taught me about reconciliation in the face of harm and welcomed me to sit in circle in their own classes and workshops.

To the many teachers who have deeply touched my life—John Paul Lederach of the Eastern Mennonite University Conflict Transformation Program, who taught me about peacebuilding in protracted interethnic conflicts; Mark Umbreit of the Center for Restorative Justice and Peacemaking at the University of Minnesota, who taught me about restorative dialogue in cases of severe political and criminal violence; the people at the Institute of Pastoral Studies at Loyola University, who taught me about spiritual guidance and the roots of nonviolence; and the people at the Fellowship of Reconciliation, who taught me how to resist oppression with a joyful and open heart.

To the hundreds of social workers, therapists, social work students, psychology graduate students, law students, residents of intentional communities, churches, theologians, mediators, wilderness and outdoor leaders, wilderness therapists, nature educators, and middle-school students, high-school students, teachers, principals, and staff at Montessori, charter, alternative, and public schools who attended my peacemaker circles and workshops and helped me grow as a teacher and peacemaker.

Most importantly, to my wife, Judy, who nurtures my soul in every possible way, connects me to the world of Montessori philosophy, and continues every day to teach me so much about the heart of council.

And to my grandchildren—may they and their own children grow up in a world at peace.

PART I

*

*The Heart
of Peacemaking*

1
Toward a Sacred Way of Being with Others

WHAT WE HAVE BEEN TAUGHT

This is a book about how to be a peacemaker. Notice that I do not say that it is about how to *become* a peacemaker. I believe that we are all peacemakers already, but we have buried our true selves under years of cultural conditioning that has made us view our relationships in hierarchical, transactional, and punitive terms. The goal is to recover our true nature, and to manifest this true nature in everything we do—in our families, our classrooms, our courts, and our communities.

We live in a culture that is *hierarchical*—that is, in which people have power over other people. We accept this as being normal and natural, as if there were no other way to live. We create spaces—classrooms, offices, courtrooms—that express this hierarchy architecturally. But there are consequences to this way of living that are worth examining.

Hierarchy is essentially unstable. In our culture, people with power over other people seek to maintain this power primarily by using punishment and the threat of punishment. This punishment can take many forms—as many forms as there are ways people can harm other people. We assert and maintain hierarchical relations by public shaming, verbal abuse, physical injury, intimidation, reduction in status, and denying basic social goods, such as education, employment, the right to vote, and liberty. We swim in a punitive ocean without even realizing it is there. We do not realize the extent to which we think in terms of punishment in our workplaces, our schools, our justice system, and our relationships with our children. We think that punishing people is normal.

In addition, power relationships are constantly being negotiated. We think that negotiation is a fair way to decide issues of power. That means that we view relationships with other people in *transactional* terms. When people are in apparent conflict with each other, we expect them to handle it transactionally—to negotiate, bargain, compromise. This is reflected in one of the key strategies of our criminal justice system—the plea bargain. We are constantly seeking to craft outcomes rather than deepen relationships.

Then we wonder why these fixes are so temporary. We see our solutions discarded, our carefully negotiated agreements abandoned in cycles of violence. We try to force people to behave, and then we are bewildered when they do not. The result is a culture in which people are oppressed by the power that others have over them—a culture in which we all oppress each other, as if it were the most natural thing in the world.

The punitive foundations of our culture, like most

cultural foundations, are expressed in myth. In our case, the foundation myth is what theologian Walter Wink has called *the myth of redemptive violence*—believing that a harm can be made right by humiliating or physically harming the offender, that violence is a necessary and appropriate response, even that such violence is healing for the victim. It is normative in our society to seek vengeance for a harm done to us. Anyone brought up in our culture has seen thousands of hours of movies and television in which the schoolyard bully is finally beaten and humiliated by his victim, or the ruthless outlaw is shot dead by the gentle sheriff. The schoolyard victim and gentle sheriff are empowered and healed by this response, and often given a sexual reward for their violence. We are all constantly tempted to reenact this mythology.

When a harm has been done in a punitive culture such as ours, founded on the myth of redemptive violence, there are, I think, four consequences.

First, it is completely rational for the person who has done the harm to try to evade responsibility for it—to lie, hide, deny, and blame others. What is the point of being accountable, if all that you get for it is punishment? What is the point of accepting responsibility for a harm you have done, if your own needs—to apologize, to make things right, to repair broken relationships—are not going to be met?

Second, a punitive system focuses on the past at the expense of the future. A punitive system is obsessed with the fact component of stories—who did what to whom in what sequence—because it is looking to single out the blameworthy participant for punishment. This means that a punitive system ignores the other components in the stories of the participants—how they feel, what they need. The system thus leaves all the participants with their stories untold, and their primary, most basic need—the need to be heard—unfulfilled. Moreover, the emphasis on punishment for the acts of the past means that the system largely ignores how to go forward into the future, how to make things right, and how to repair and restore broken bonds of trust in the community.

Third, a punitive system imposes a kind of Manichaeism—a belief that the world consists of two powers, good and evil, light and dark, easily distinguished, in constant battle. This Manichaean mythology pervades our criminal justice system and most of our thinking. We worry about the facts because we believe the facts will show us how to apportion blame. When people are in conflict, we attempt to punctuate their ongoing relationship, and thus determine who is the one to be punished. We feel compelled to distinguish bad guys from good guys, because only in this way can we make sure that bad guys get what they deserve. And if we fail at punctuating the interaction, we often throw up our hands and punish both.

Fourth, our culture views punishment in transactional terms. The very terms we use— giving people what they *deserve*—embodies a transactional view. Being punished for having harmed someone is very much like a business transaction. The punishment is frequently negotiated. For example, punishment may be lessened in exchange for an admission or an apology—often a meaningless apology, with no intent to repair the harm or make things right. The transactional nature of punishment is also captured in the saying, *Don't do the crime if you can't do the time.* Think about the converse:

If you can do the time, then hell, you might as well do the crime.

This means that the decision to harm another person is reduced to a calculus that does not involve the other person at all—only the harmer and the justice system. This means, too, that someone who has harmed another person is not put face-to-face with the harm that has been done—the physical injury, the fear, the loss of safety, the inconvenience suffered by the person harmed. The harmer does not have to deal with the person harmed at all. The harmer is involved only in negotiating with the justice system for the best possible deal.

HOW WE BREAK FREE

Because we have been brought up in a hierarchical, punitive, and transactional culture, we are ourselves hierarchical, punitive, and transactional in our lives, in how we deal with others, and in how we view ourselves. Living in this way has significant costs in human happiness. We find it difficult to form deep openhearted human relationships; we enter into seemingly endless cycles of violence and retribution; we constantly seek but never quite find the community of our best imagination—egalitarian, liberating, and transformational. We fail to walk in beauty.

But there is an alternative—a way to relate to each other in a *sacred* way, which focuses on repair, restoration, and healing.

Before King Solomon became King of Israel, he had a dream. In this dream, God offered to grant him anything he wished—wealth, power, many wives. What Solomon chose instead is usually translated as *wisdom* or *understanding*. But the original Hebrew term for what Solomon desired is *lev sho-mea*, which literally means *a listening heart*.

Saint Francis of Assisi, too, spoke of the need for a "transformed and undefended heart." I believe that a listening heart and an undefended heart amount to the same thing. We have erected barricades around our hearts, so that we cannot hear each other. We have been systematically taught in our culture not to listen to each other. We must learn to listen, and we do that by tearing down the walls we have built.

When I was being trained in active nonviolence by the Fellowship of Reconciliation, we were taught that, when entering a potentially confrontational situation, the first thing we needed to do was to *disarm ourselves*. Everything in this book about peacemaking is summed up in such words. We must learn to have a listening heart; we must learn to have an undefended heart; we must disarm ourselves. And then we can begin to disarm others.

We will begin this book with a practice of peacemaking founded in what has been variously called *council, circle, peace circle, peacemaking circle, talking circle,* and any number of other names. The idea of council is very simple and can be described in a few sentences. In council people sit in a circle and pass around what is called a *talking stick*. Whoever holds the talking stick gets to speak, and everybody else listens. There are no interruptions, no questions, no challenges, no comments. People speak one at a time, in turn, honestly from their hearts, and they listen devoutly with their hearts to each person who speaks. The effect can be miraculous.

But, as I will have occasion to note in the course of this book, simple does not mean easy. The few principles I talk about—and their extension into other areas of life and conflict—must be applied regularly, every day, in every encounter. Because we will all struggle and often fail, we must maintain the warrior virtues of transparency, vulnerability, courage, and accountability. We must put ourselves out there, hand our talking stick to everyone we meet, and strive to walk in beauty every day.

2
The Geography of Hierarchy

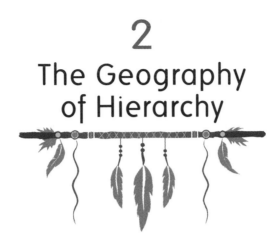

Often, when I begin to teach a class or seminar on peacemaking, I find the room set up in a certain way. There is a lectern in the front of the room, and often a table as well. As I stand behind the lectern, I see rows of seats, one after the other, all facing the front of the room. Behind me there is a board to write on, and usually a projection screen. On the lectern may be devices for controlling the lights, a computer, a DVD player, a projector.

When everyone is seated, I look out over the rows of faces, and I say, "I want to try something with you. I would like everyone to hold up their right hand." Almost always, everyone complies. If someone hesitates, I say, "Come on, everyone, please. Thank you." That always works.

Then I tell everyone to put down their right hands and raise their left hands. This time everyone does, even those who hesitated before. Then I tell them to put down their left hands and, on the count of three, to clap their hands together, twice. Everyone always does.

Then I say, "Now that looked really foolish. Why did you do that?" The conversation that follows usually goes like this:

"Because you told us to."

"That's true. But why did you do what I told you?"

There is usually some mumbling at this point, until someone says, "Because you're the authority."

And I say, "How did you know I was the authority?"

After some discussion, we conclude that they knew I was the authority because *the geography of the room created hierarchy.* I am standing and they are sitting, so I am higher than they are. I can see all of them, but they cannot see each other. I have a lectern and table as a barricade between us. I can talk whenever I want, and they have to ask permission to speak. I have control of all the communication technology—the board, the screen, the projector. I have power because of the nature of the space we occupy.

We then spend a little time talking about the way geography creates hierarchy in other settings—in a courtroom, for example. The judge sits up high, behind a barricade, wearing special judge clothing, surrounded by subordinates performing mysterious tasks. No one can even approach the judge without asking permission. There is no doubt who is in charge in a courtroom. Participants come up with other examples—an executive in an office, sitting in a luxurious chair behind a large desk; their academic advisor in a cluttered office filled with books representing many years of learning.

In all these cases, geography normalizes the idea that

some people are more important than others and therefore have a voice that carries more weight than the voices of other people. So finally we decide that we will deliberately *subvert hierarchy.* We will move all the chairs around and sit in a circle.

3
The Components of Council

There are three simple things that make council special as a way of meeting together, making decisions, solving problems, dealing with conflicts, and building community:

◇ Sitting in a circle
◇ Beginning and ending with a ceremony
◇ Using a talking stick

CIRCLE

Sitting in a circle is the first of these. There are practical reasons for sitting in a circle. Everyone can see everyone else. No one is in front, and no one can hide in the back. But the circle is symbolic as well. The circle indicates the equality of all who sit together. There is no head of the table. Everyone's voice carries as much weight as the voice of everyone else. Everyone is out front, equally accountable for their words.

The world is filled with circles. The sun is a circle; the

moon becomes a circle over and over again—that is, in a cycle, a circle. For most of our history humans have lived, not in the square sharp-cornered containers in which we live now, but rather in circular houses, often explicitly homologized to a circular cosmos. The year and its seasons go in a circle. Our lives go in a circle. We all follow in the footsteps of our elders and teachers who have gone before us; I am getting old now, but I have grandchildren who are coming after me.

And the circle binds us to our ancestors. Whoever you are, wherever your people came from, whatever the color of your skin, your ancestors sat in a circle to meet together, make decisions, solve problems, deal with conflicts, and sing the songs and tell the stories that sustained and nurtured their communities.

Most important, sitting in a circle creates a special space— a safe space, what many indigenous people would call a *sacred space*. The council circle takes place in a special space that differs from our ordinary space. In the sacred space of council, it is possible to speak honestly without embarrassment; it is a place where confidences are kept; it is where decisions are made and peacemaking takes place. This is the space inside the circle, within which people listen to each other devoutly and give each other the courage to speak honestly from their hearts. This space is very different from the space outside the circle—a space where people interrupt each other, do not listen to each other, are rude to each other.

The next time you attend a meeting—a business meeting, for example, or a meeting of a community group—observe how people behave. People arrive with their opinions already formed and may carry with them notes of their talking points so that they do not forget to say something they think is important. People interrupt each other. People shift about impatiently while others are speaking. People do not pause after someone has finished speaking, to show that they are thinking about what that person has said. Instead, people start speaking immediately after someone has finished—indeed, not just when someone has finished, but even when someone simply pauses to take a breath or think about what to say next. The loudest or most aggressive talkers dominate the meeting; shy people may get no opportunity to speak at all.

That is how people act *out there,* outside the sacred circle. But *inside* the council circle, where we can all see each other, where we take turns speaking, we create a space that is filled with respect and receptivity for what everyone has to say. Inside this circle, we create a *sacred* space—a space that is safe for speaking, because it is a space for listening. Take a deep breath. Inside the circle, we are home.

There are a number of ways to demarcate the separate and sacred nature of the council space. The council may be held in a special place—a grove of trees, by the bank of a river, on top of a large rock, in a cave. A number of classrooms that use council have a *peace table* in one corner. This special place for peacemaking might also have a way of marking the number of times that the place has seen friendships renewed and breaches healed—marks on a stick, a pile of stones—that makes the table into a place of power.

In a circle, too, the gaze of all the participants is naturally oriented not only toward whoever is speaking but also toward the center of the circle. The sacred nature of the circle can be enhanced by making an altar or *council table* at the center.

Making the altar can be a rotating responsibility among the participants, or the altar can be made by those who are moved to do so on any particular occasion. Again, there are numerous variations. The altar can contain flowers, stones, fallen leaves, feathers, or branches that have been gathered before the council. An altar of special significance can be made by each participant placing in the center an object that has personal meaning—a photograph, key chain, pocket knife, memento—or that symbolizes the issues to be discussed at council.

Or again, if council is held outdoors in an appropriate place and especially for evening councils, the center can be marked by a fire—not the cooking fire, but a special and separate fire. There is something primal about sharing the warmth and light of a fire in the darkness. The glowing fire, the sense of safety, the intimacy and privacy of the darkness seem to lead people to share more of their secret selves than they might do in the harsher daylight. The fire represents a deep and centered place, the heart of everything, the unity for which the circle strives.

But most important is this. *Any time you listen devoutly to another you have created a sacred space.* The circle exists wherever people hold the intention of sitting in council together. Two people can be in council; you can be in council with yourself.

CEREMONY

The second thing that makes council or circle special as a way of meeting together, making decisions, solving problems, dealing with conflicts, and building community is that it begins and ends with a *ceremony*. Just as sitting in a circle creates a special space, a safe space, a *sacred* space, the use of a ceremony creates a special kind of *time*—a special time, a safe time, a sacred time.

I often burn sage as part of the ceremony. I do this because it was the way I was taught, and I honor my teachers by using the ceremony they taught me. I also do this because I think that sage teaches several important lessons.

The sage bush is actually an unprepossessing little plant— scruffy looking, low to the ground, with twisted branches and plain leathery leaves. Yet after a rainstorm, you can smell the sage for miles across the desert. And many indigenous people of North America believe that the fragrant smoke of burning sage is healing, protective, and purifying. They bathe in the smoke of burning sage, by putting some on top of the hot rocks in the sweat lodge, or burning some in a bowl or shell and directing the smoke over their bodies with their hand or a feather.

Here is something about sage you may not know. When making a fire by rubbing sticks together, the pointed bottom of a vertical spindle fits into a notch on a flat baseboard. When the spindle is rotated very rapidly, whether between the hands or by using a bow, the resulting friction causes two things to happen: a fine powder rubs off into the notch, and that fine powder becomes hotter and hotter until it becomes a glowing ember. That ember is then transferred into a nest of kindling to start the fire. Although it takes some work to make a nice straight spindle, the wood of the sage bush makes a wonderful fire kit, producing both heat and an ignitable powder.

So here is this short, scruffy, unprepossessing bush, whose leaves not only produce a smoke that is healing, protective, and purifying, but whose wood also creates the fire that burns the leaves to make that healing, protective, and purifying smoke. And it does all this for free.

When I am the one charged with the opening ceremony, I like to recite this poem by neopagan and ecofeminist pioneer Starhawk:

> *If we have courage, we shall be healers*
> *Like the sun we shall rise.*
> *If we have courage, we shall be healers*
> *Like the sun we shall rise.*
> *We are alive as the earth is alive.*
> *We have the power to live all our freedom.*

I put some sage onto an abalone shell, light the sage, and bathe in its smoke. I say a few words of gratitude for the chance to gather together in council with others. I pass the shell to the person sitting on my left—clockwise, in the direction of the sun—and the shell, with the burning sage, makes its way around the circle. People can bathe in the smoke, using their hands to direct the smoke over their heads, onto their bodies, and over their shoulders, to cleanse away the burdens they might have brought into the council circle. They can simply smell the fragrance of the smoke, or smell it and think of the earth, who gives us the healing plants for free. They can just silently pass the shell on to the next person, or say some brief words. Some choose to say words from their own tradition; one woman, a devout

Catholic, made the sign of the cross with the shell and its smoking sage.

Here, as always, there are many different ways. Some indigenous peoples believe that it is rude to blow on the burning sage with breath from your mouth, so that participants in a circle use a feather—often a sacred eagle feather—to move the smoke. Others believe that only an appropriate elder can touch a sacred feather, so the elder moves around the circle, bathing each participant with the smoke from the burning sage.

I would be remiss not to mention three problems with burning sage indoors in an institutional setting such as a classroom. First, there is a remote but real possibility of setting off a smoke detector, activating the classroom sprinkler system, and triggering an automatic call to the fire department. This has never happened to me, but it has happened to someone I know, to her great embarrassment. Second, we need to be alert to the possible presence of people with allergies or asthma who might react to breathing the smoke in an enclosed space. The third problem was unexpected. We were burning sage before council during my university class in restorative justice when the campus police burst in, saying that they had received complaints that people were smoking marijuana in the classroom. It took a few minutes to get that one straightened out.

I have seen a wide variety of opening ceremonies used, from the simple to the elaborate. If a community meets regularly in council, ceremonies appropriate to that community will grow spontaneously and organically. Simply saying to another person who is familiar with council, *Hey, let's circle up on this,* is a commitment to take the time to listen to the other devoutly and to speak honestly to the other from the heart. The ceremony can be simply lighting a candle. Words can be spoken, either formalized or spontaneous, ranging from *We are now in council* to more elaborate invocations. The words can be spoken by one of the participants, or by everyone together. If the council is held with the same participants on a regular basis—for example, each morning, or once a week—the participants may take turns beginning the council or creating opening ceremonies. In one school community, the students took turns bringing in and reading poems that were meaningful to them.

Be creative with your ceremonies. Think of all the ways you can symbolize the passage from ordinary into sacred time—crossing a threshold, lighting a candle, circling clockwise, drumming, washing your hands, putting on special clothes, saying words of gratitude, bathing in sage smoke, and many more. Along with ceremony, this sense of a special and sacred time can be enhanced by coordinating council with a special and sacred time of the day, such as sunrise or sunset, or seasonally at solstice or equinox, or on the night when the Evening Star first becomes visible.

Ceremonies can range from the quick and simple to the elaborate and formalized. When people are accustomed to council, it is not unusual to hear someone say: *An issue has come up. Let's circle up for a minute and deal with it.* In one middle school class that uses council on a regular basis, students had been formed into four-person teams to work on a project. One group had been quarrelsome and unproductive, and the teacher was delighted to hear one of the students spontaneously say: *We're not getting anywhere. We need to go get the stick.*

There is a delicate balance between creating a sense of formality, solemnity, and tradition, on the one hand, and spontaneity, creativity, and openheartedness on the other. I was in a circle once with such an elaborate opening ceremony that the young apprentice doing the ceremony was continually interrupted by audible whispers from her mentor about sections of the ceremony she had forgotten or not done quite right. This was not a good model for spontaneity of expression or for an openhearted acceptance of what comes from the heart.

Some writers have proposed lengthy ceremonial statements to be used by each participant when passing the talking stick to the next speaker—for example, *Do you love yourself enough to speak and listen with your heart to your co-hearts in this circle? If so, can you tell us . . . ?* Some participants may have difficulty memorizing such formulas and may wind up spending a lot of time trying to get the formula straight in their minds, and worrying they will mess it up, rather than listening with their hearts to the person speaking on their right.

The purpose of any ceremony—simple or elaborate—is to show that the time of council is different from ordinary time. Just as sitting in circle creates a sacred space, the opening ceremony creates a sacred time. *Out there* we are in a hurry; *out there* we have an agenda, things to do, electronic devices with an alarm function. *Out there* we are interested in getting things done, achieving an outcome, creating a product. But in sacred time there is no rush; there is nothing particular to be accomplished; we are in no hurry. We are immersed in *pure process.*

In the sacred time of council, created by the ceremony, there is no need to follow an agenda, make a decision, formulate a plan, come up with a solution, craft an agreement. Sacred time is not linear but rather is circular. In sacred time, things recur but perhaps each time in a different light. Spirit cannot be rushed or scheduled. In sacred time, the circle waits patiently for spirit to speak. Being in sacred time with others teaches us these two lessons:

How to be comfortable with silence. It is important to let people gather their thoughts or wait for spirit to speak through them or just pause between sentences. If you are in the sacred time of council, there is no hurry to get anywhere in particular. We can listen devoutly to the silence just as we would listen to someone speaking. Simply sharing sacred time with another person builds and deepens relationships.

How to be comfortable with talking. Not everyone gets right to the point or to what you think the point should be. Sometimes people need to talk their way toward their truth. Sometimes people are thinking out loud. Sometimes people are just building rapport, getting comfortable, testing the waters. There is no rush because, in sacred time, there is nowhere you need to get to.

A social worker came to an Indian reservation intending to help build a mental health clinic. She was told that she would accomplish nothing without the approval of a certain elder who was held in great respect by the community. So late one afternoon she went to the elder's house, bringing an appropriate gift of tobacco. When she knocked on the door, the elder's wife told the social worker that her husband was out back. The social worker went into the backyard and saw the elder sitting in a lawn chair, looking out over the hills. She offered him the tobacco, which he accepted silently, gesturing toward a lawn chair next to his. For the next hour and a half, the social worker sat silently next to the elder as they both watched the sun slowly set behind the hills. When the sun had set completely, the elder turned toward the social worker and said, "I think we will be able to work together."

TALKING STICK

The third thing that makes council or circle special as a way of meeting together, making decisions, solving problems, dealing with conflicts, and building community is the *talking stick*. The rule of the talking stick is simple: *Whoever holds the stick gets to speak, and everyone else listens.* The stick is passed around the circle, and each person holds it in turn.

My practice has always been to pass the stick around the circle clockwise. I do that because that is the direction the sun travels from rising to setting, at least in the northern hemisphere, and that is the way I was taught. Other people may pass the stick in a counterclockwise direction, or sometimes one way and sometimes the other. As with many things, there is no one way to do it.

The rule of the talking stick is simple, but that does not mean it is easy. In fact, the rule is quite difficult to follow, because we have been systematically taught in our culture not to listen to each other.

My talking stick is a rawhide rattle that I made and decorated myself. I have carried that rattle with me on my vision quests in the desert, in order to call the spirits. One day I had the rattle with me when some people asked me to help them sit in council together, and we used the rattle as our talking stick. We had a wonderful and deeply openhearted circle, and I started to use the rattle in every circle I could. That talking stick has now been held by thousands of people, all of whom had the courage to hold that stick and speak honestly from their hearts. As a result, all that courage has passed into the stick, and the stick is now very powerful.

The talking stick can be anything—a stick, a rock, a statue, a feather, a ballpoint pen, a fork picked up off the table. Some people use the term *talking piece* instead of *talking stick* to reflect the fact that what is passed around the circle does not need to be a stick at all. The stick can be specially made and decorated, an object which is personal or sacred or symbolic, simple or elaborate, or it can be expedient—a rock picked up on the spur of the moment, a coffee cup, a key ring. The purpose of council is to create a safe space in which people can simply talk honestly and sincerely with each other. The talking stick is a way of providing some of that safety; a participant can speak without being interrupted or argued with. Indeed, the talking stick can supply courage to the shy and steadiness to the flighty; it symbolizes the responsibility of speech, the courage of the true speaker, the importance of truth.

When a group of people meet in council on a regular basis they may decide to have a stick they make together and keep in a special place. For example, a class in school may make their own communal talking stick, with everyone contributing something to its decoration—a bead, a feather, a piece of an old baby blanket kept for many years. In fact, taking down such a stick from its special place may be part of the ceremony that is used to open a council session; or two people, finding themselves in apparent conflict, may both go to the special place and take down the stick together, in order to symbolize their entry into the sacred space and time of circle. This can be the briefest of opening ceremonies: *Hey, we're not getting anywhere. Let's go get the stick.*

Sometimes there is no specially made stick available, and the stick is something used spontaneously. I was once eating dinner with my wife, a Montessori directress and consultant, who has used council regularly in her classroom and in her school. She was telling me about her day, and I was, I confess, not paying attention very well. Suddenly, she stopped speaking, looked at me, and slapped her hand on the table. "Dammit, Steve," she said, "you are not listening devoutly with your heart!" I immediately picked up a fork, handed it to her, and that became our talking stick.

The talking stick is miraculous. As a practical matter, the stick creates order. People cannot interrupt each other or try to shout over each other. People have to wait their turn, no matter how strongly they feel about what was just said. The talking stick empowers the shy and deferential to speak and keeps the loud and overbearing from dominating the discussion. The fact that people must wait for the stick to travel around the circle means that they cannot react immediately to something they disagree with. Instead they must first listen to what other people have to say, which often frames the statement in new and enlightening ways. The stick discourages personal confrontation and encourages group process.

But more than that is involved. The process of passing the stick is deeply and profoundly human. The stick taps into a primal way of being together. I have seen people stroke the stick as they spoke or hold it next to their hearts, as if gathering courage from it. People use as talking sticks things that are deeply meaningful to them personally. One of my friends uses the decorated staff he carries as a road chief in the Native American Church; another uses a small Buddha statue carved from green jade. I urge you to find or make your own talking stick, and carry it with you. Treat it with respect, bathe it in the smoke of sage; keep it on your home altar if you have one. Have it blessed; give it power. Create a ceremony to transform a decorated stick into a talking stick.

In fact, the stick does not have to be visible at all; you can carry with you an *invisible talking stick*. We will talk about that later.

4
The Intentions of Council

You are sitting in council, watching the talking stick make its way around the circle, coming closer and closer to you. What are you doing?

It is my guess that, if you are like most people, you are thinking about what you are going to say. You are trying to remember what George said when he had the stick because George was just so totally wrong that he needs to be set straight about a few things. You come up with a really good turn of phrase, so you keep trying to remember it to use when you speak. You make a mental list of all the really important points you need to make so you don't forget anything. You mentally rehearse what you are going to say so it comes out just right when you finally—*finally*—hold the stick and get to speak. You wish you could make notes on a piece of paper.

And while all this is going on, what are you *not* doing? That's right. You are not listening.

As I said earlier, we have been systematically taught in our culture not to listen to each other or to listen selectively solely to formulate a response. We have been taught that we must be prepared to respond, that we must know what we are going to say, so that we do not sound hesitant or foolish. That is why it has been said that in our culture when two people are talking together, one is speaking and the other is not listening but *reloading*.

For that reason, there are what we call *the four intentions of council;* that is, we enter into the council circle *intending* to do these four things:

◊ Speak honestly from our hearts
◊ Listen devoutly with our hearts
◊ Speak spontaneously
◊ Be of lean expression

Let's look at these one at a time.

SPEAKING HONESTLY FROM THE HEART

In my classes and seminars, I often announce that I have been married to the same woman for almost fifty years, and I offer some free advice on how to have a successful long-term relationship: *When you're right, apologize.* It may take a moment for people to get the joke, and then I say: *Because it's not about being right; it's about the relationship.*

The same thing is true for council. It's not about being right. It's about the relationship. We enter into the council circle intending to speak honestly from our hearts, to speak our own truth with humility. We are not in council to be right; we are there to deepen our relationships by speaking our truth. We are not there to fix people, save people, give people advice, or set people straight. We are not there to show that we are smarter or better or wiser or *righter* than other people. We are there to speak honestly from our hearts.

The heart, with which we speak and listen in council, is the center of our being, that which integrates passion and energy. To speak from the heart is to speak one's truth, honestly, sincerely, and with humility. This can be very difficult. It is risky, and it requires courage.

This means that just about everything we say in council begins with the pronoun *I*. I do not know what is in your heart, until you tell me. When I begin a statement with *you*, I am being presumptuous. I am trying to tell you what is in your heart, not in mine. But when I begin a statement with *I*, I am trying to tell you about my truth, not yours. We say: *I think, I believe, I understand* . . . and most importantly, *I feel, I need* . . .

I also recommend getting rid of the word *but*. When I say: *John had a very interesting idea, but I think* . . . I am sweeping away John's idea from the center of the circle and putting my idea in its place. When I say: *John had a very interesting idea, and I would like to add this thought* . . . I am putting my idea next to John's in the center of the circle. Are we better off with one idea or with two ideas?

There are no rules about what may be spoken from the heart. It can be a memory, a song, or silence. But speaking from the heart is always, in some sense, speaking our stories— stories of our day, stories of our hopes and fears and regrets, stories of our lives. We tell stories about the conflicts we hope to heal and the decisions we have to make. When we sit in sacred time, when we are not in a hurry, when we have no place in particular we are going, human beings have always opened their hearts by telling their stories. *This is my story,* we say. *This is my vision, this is my dream, this is my truth, this is my sacred song.*

It takes great courage to speak our truths with humility. But what is it we are afraid of? Poet and activist Audre Lorde put it best: we fear contempt, censure, the harsh light of scrutiny, judgment; we fear recognition, challenge, annihilation. But most of all, she said, we fear the visibility without which we cannot truly live. When she was diagnosed with the breast cancer that eventually killed her, she wrote:

> I was going to die, if not sooner then later, whether or not I had ever spoken myself. My silences had not protected me. Your silence will not protect you. . . . What are the words you do not yet have? What do you need to say?

The purpose of the sacred space and time within the council circle is to provide the safety within which these words can be, perhaps for the first time, spoken and heard.

LISTENING DEVOUTLY WITH THE HEART

The second intention of council is to listen devoutly with the heart. Each participant has to intend to *listen*—suspending criticism, refraining from argument, not preparing a response, not judging appearances. This is remarkably difficult; it goes against all our ingrained habits of conversation.

Listening devoutly from the heart has two intertwined components—listening devoutly and listening with the heart. The use of the term *devoutly* is not simply metaphoric. As in a Quaker meeting, the proper attitude is a reverential awareness that it is spirit addressing us through each speaker. Call it whatever makes sense to you—spirit, the spirits, collective wisdom. But there is not a doubt in my mind that the collective wisdom of the council is a thousand times greater than the wisdom of any one participant.

Have you ever had the experience of speaking with someone you thought was . . . well, a fool; and then, amazingly, the person said something perceptive, insightful, astute? Or it may be, in a circle concerned with discerning the best way forward in a situation of conflict, the process may be unexpectedly illuminated by someone's apparently unrelated story of once having been lost in the woods. The lesson is this: *You never know where wisdom is going to come from.* And as we will see in a moment, it might even come from you, so you had best get out of the way.

And we listen devoutly *with our heart.* We do not listen with our critical analysis or moral judgment or intellectual assessment. When someone is speaking to us from the heart, the only organ we have that can hear what is being said is our own listening heart—our own *lev shomea,* which is wisdom.

Rachel Naomi Remen, a medical doctor, has this to say in her wonderful book *Kitchen Table Wisdom:*

I suspect that the most basic and powerful way to connect to another person is to listen. Just listen. Perhaps the most important thing we ever give each other is our attention. And especially if it's given from the heart. When people are talking, there's no need to do anything but receive them. Just take them in. Listen to what they're saying. Care about it. Most times caring about it is even more important than understanding it. Most of us don't value ourselves or our love enough to know this.

We do not listen to people because they are interesting. They are interesting because we listen to them, and the more deeply we listen the more interesting they become. There is an old Jewish saying: "God loves stories, so he created people." Everyone has a story, every story is interesting, and every story is—in its own way—true.

Think of your own needs when you are angry or frustrated or upset. The last thing you need is for someone to tell you to calm down, not feel the way you feel. The last thing you need is for someone to give you advice, or tell you how their uncle dealt with a similar problem, or recommend a self-help book for you to read. What you need more than anything else at that moment is *to be heard*. You need to tell your story to someone who will listen devoutly with his or her heart.

When we listen with our heart, we were also listening with *our whole body,* as if our body were an antenna or satellite dish, turning toward the speaker, opening up our body as our heart opens. Listening is a sort of meditative practice— letting the mind be calm, not planning, not responding, not thinking. True listening is like Zen no-mind, pure presence and awareness. Listening is a process of emptying yourself.

There is an exercise that I often do in my workshops and seminars that I call the *not-listening exercise.* I talk about the fact that everyone has, somewhere, a *special place*—a place where they have experienced joy, contentment, love, peace, a sense of harmony. The place may be real or imaginary; it may be a place where they have lived or traveled or visited; it may be a place they have dreamed. Then the group is divided up into pairs. I ask the first person in each pair to tell the second person all about this special place, in as much detail as they can, describing how they found it, what it looks like, how it makes them feel.

And I ask the second person in each pair *not to listen.*

It is remarkable to watch people not listening. As the first person speaks, sometimes with great emotion, about their special place, the not-listeners cross their arms and legs, gaze off into space, check their cell phones, nod to others in the room, rummage through their bags and briefcases, hum softly, stare out the window—in other words, behave very much like bored adolescents.

I usually stop the exercise after just a few minutes and ask the participants about their experience. I ask them to describe the ways in which the not-listeners were visibly not listening—the closed body posture, the eyes turned away, the lack of response. I ask the speakers in each pair to describe their feelings, and they talk about their frustration, their anger, their sense of humiliation. But always the speakers all come down to the same thing. *They wanted to stop speaking.*

Often the discussion turns to what has been called *active listening,* in which people are taught how to mimic real listening—showing an open body posture, making periodic and culturally appropriate eye contact, nodding and occasionally interjecting an *mm-hmm*—all of which can be done even while paying no attention at all.

So now the participants switch places. The not-listeners get to tell about their special places, and I ask the previous speakers now to do nothing but listen, as intently as they can, *devoutly with their hearts.*

The transformation is remarkable. Bodies open like flowers, arms and legs uncross, the listeners lean forward so as not to miss a word, eyes engage, and every gesture of the listener communicates interest, curiosity, and sympathy. The speakers open their hearts in the presence of such listening, and the stories just tumble out. It is wonderful to watch. When I end the exercise, people hug.

Again I ask the participants about their experience. The speakers describe their feeling of acceptance and encouragement. The listeners were often completely unaware of their own postures and gestures; they were too busy listening. And they would say: The story was so *interesting.*

Listening devoutly with the heart is not tiring. In fact, like meditation, it is refreshing. I have several times sat in council with groups of law students. After one such circle, one of the students told me that she had been trained in her law classes constantly to critique in her mind what another person was saying: *That's a bad argument. I can refute it like this. Omigod, where did he find that case? Wait, I've got a better case I can cite.* Listening like that—with critical analysis and moral judgment—was all hard work. But when she listened devoutly, instead of mentally counterattacking, she did not have to do all that work. She could, she said, just be present, open, relaxed, receptive, listening—not working.

SPEAKING SPONTANEOUSLY

The intention to be spontaneous means simply that each participant does not plan ahead what to say but speaks without preparation. Spontaneity is in many ways a natural result of listening devoutly; when you are really listening, you are not preparing. Conversely, an intention to be spontaneous when we speak is a means to allow us to listen without distraction.

Spontaneity is a very difficult intention for many participants. We probably would all have to admit that most of the time, when we are talking with someone else, we are not so much listening as patiently—or impatiently—waiting our turn to speak. Moreover, while we are listening in council we think of things we want to say, important things, meaningful and impressive things that we don't want to forget; so we constantly make mental notes of the topics to cover when it is our turn.

But spontaneity in council means more than avoiding distraction while listening. The intention to be spontaneous is a form of surrender to the process—a trust that you will say what needs to be said *at that moment*. The remarkable experience of finding oneself speaking spontaneously from the heart, without notes or preparation or rehearsal, is again often stated in spiritual terms—that the speaker is moved by spirit, or spirit is speaking *through* the participant.

In fact, spontaneity includes spontaneous *silence*—the

willingness simply to pass the talking stick—if one finds that one has, on that round, nothing to say. Spontaneous silence and the *acceptance* of spontaneous silence are also ways of trusting the process. The assumption is that the individual participant is not necessarily responsible for making a point to the council; what *needs* to be said will get said by someone or by spirit, and spontaneously.

Here we learn a great lesson from the American Quaker meeting house. The Society of Friends was founded around 1647 by George Fox, who preached the personal immediacy of Christian experience. The Spirit of Christ, he said, is the light within, "the light that lightens everyman." Thus the word of Christ is within each individual. "The word is nigh thee," Fox wrote, "in thy mouth and in thy heart." And thus: "You will say, Christ saith this, and the apostles say that; but what canst thou say?" In this spirit, Quaker meetings are without clergy, and often silent, as each participant waits upon the word in order to give testimony, seeking to speak lucidly and concisely, responding to a divine opening. That is how we strive to speak in council—letting the sacred spirit of peacemaking within us speak our truth with humility.

It is a remarkable experience to open up the heart and speak spontaneously. To hear honest, simple eloquence come forth from your own heart is one of the miracles of council.

BEING OF LEAN EXPRESSION

Concision or *lean expression* is, among other things, a courtesy to the other council participants. The term means that the speaker avoids digressions and long-windedness. More important, the intention to be concise interacts with spontaneity: the speaker trusts the process enough to feel that what is said is enough.

I think this point is worth emphasizing. Both spontaneity and concision are expressions of trust and abandonment of ego. The speaker trusts that spirit—or whatever you want to call the web of connections that move the council forward toward an often unapprehended goal—will make things right at the end.

It may take some time for people to come to lean expression. Sometimes participants will grasp the stick for dear life and just keep talking. Such people have been taught—probably repeatedly—that, unless they keep talking, *no one will listen to them*. Sometimes it is the sheer exhilaration of being listened to, perhaps for the first time. In council this impulse to speak at length is self-healing. When people realize that they are really being heard, that the circle is leaning forward to hear their heart speak to them, then concision comes naturally. People learn that it is not the individual but the circle that speaks, and they become willing to play their own natural part.

THE UNITY OF THE INTENTIONS

In the sacred space and time of council, the four intentions are actually an interactive whole. Listening and speaking are deeply intertwined. People speak honestly from their hearts when they are listened to, when the listener creates a safe and sacred space within which honest speaking can take place. Conversely, honest speaking *compels listening*. When we speak honestly from our hearts, spontaneously and without preparation, we are also devoutly listening to our own best selves, and letting its spirit speak through us. And here *through* is the operative term; it is almost always ego—the hierarchical sense of being smarter, knowing more, being able to control and advise and fix—that stands between us and our open hearts and the open hearts of others. Remove that barrier; give yourself over without ego to the process of council, and peacemaking can begin.

5
Ensuring Safety

I have said that circle is a special place, a safe space, a *sacred* space within which you can speak honestly from your heart. And of course you do not believe me.

I would bet that at some point someone has said to you: *It's all right. You can tell me the truth. You won't get into trouble.* And then you told the truth, and of course you got into trouble. Just ask any adolescent.

There are three agreements that people in council can make that will make the participants feel safe enough to speak their truth:

◇ Confidentiality
◇ Acceptability of silence
◇ Affirmation

CONFIDENTIALITY

First, everyone can agree that council is *confidential*. What is said in council stays in council; nothing said within the circle leaves the circle. It may be worthwhile to ask each person in the circle individually if he or she agrees to this. It's that important.

There are—I think rarely—good reasons to break the agreement of confidentiality. If there is a chance of such circumstances occurring, council participants should discuss the issue ahead of time. For example, some participants may be mandated reporters, and a circle with minors may trigger a reporting obligation. In some jurisdictions a credible threat of immediate violence, including a threat of suicide, may trigger an obligation to call for intervention. I have heard the acronym DASH used in this connection, meaning drugs, abuse, suicide, and homicide.

Confidentiality is probably the single most important guideline for good councils. People simply will not speak their hearts if they fear repercussions outside the sacred council space. Participants may need reassurance on this point from time to time. In an established circle it is to be hoped that confidentiality will have been so fully internalized as a norm that such reassurances become unnecessary.

I was doing a participatory presentation of council at a national teachers' conference. All the presentations were being video recorded for later sale to members—except mine. We were going to be in circle together, and that meant no recording devices of any kind. The videographer put up a brief fuss and then left.

The requirement of confidentiality should not preclude people from talking *about* what happened in council. Often things happen in council that are interesting, or sad, or illuminating, and people often want—and should be allowed—

to share these experiences with others. What is important here is sensitivity to the principles of privacy and protection that underlie the idea of confidentiality. Names or any other identifying information should not be revealed, and circumstantial information that might let these be guessed should also be omitted.

And there are circumstances under which it makes sense for council matters to be discussed outside of council *with permission*—for example, *John, I'd like to talk with you privately about something you said in council. Can we circle up on that?* What then takes place can be a *two-person council*, informed by the intention of both participants to listen devoutly to each other, and to maintain the confidentiality of that circle. Since the two speakers find themselves in council, there is no breach of council confidentiality. To act otherwise—to use the discussion as a way to throw a council statement back in the speaker's face—would then be to have breached the sacred space.

ACCEPTABILITY OF SILENCE

Second, everyone can agree that *silence is always acceptable.* No one should ever be pressured to participate. No one has to explain silence. Indeed, silence may be the most salient contribution a person can make. Moreover, no one should ever be made to feel ashamed at awkwardness or reluctance. It should be made clear that to say, *I'm just not comfortable disclosing myself right now, so I think I'll pass,* or simply to pass the stick in silence is as honest and courageous as any other disclosure and should be honored.

If people feel pressured to speak or to speak in a way that is not their way of speaking or to be self-revealing in a way that makes them uncomfortable, then of course a hierarchy has been erected, the speaker has been subordinated to the demands of the group, and people are not in council at all.

In fact, there is any number of very good reasons to pass the stick without speaking. Someone may already have said what you were going to say, and you see no reason to repeat it. You may in fact have nothing to say at that particular moment. You may want the stick to go around the circle once or a few times more to get a better sense of what the circle needs from you. And offering the gift of silence may be the very best thing you can offer the circle *at that moment.* You may have correctly sensed that everyone needs just a little silence, and that silence is your contribution. Indeed, silence may be the most profound and eloquent expression of what you are trying to say.

Participants do not give up their right to speak by passing the stick in silence; there is always another round or another opportunity to speak. If someone in the circle does not wish to speak when handed the stick, I suggest that the person still hold onto the stick for a moment or two before passing it to the next person. There are two reasons for that suggestion. Holding the stick for a moment—rather than passing it to the next person like a hot potato—shows respect for the stick and for the circle process. Even more important, when you hold the stick you may discover that, contrary to what you believed a moment before, you do have something to say and that holding the stick has freed it from your fear or uncertainty and placed it on your tongue.

It is important to be alert for any coerciveness in the council session. Many people are unused to speaking from the heart, feel embarrassed or intimidated or awkward or simply have a greater need for privacy than others in the circle. It is very easy for such people in the circle to feel pressured into being more forthcoming than they really want to be *at that moment.*

Any coerced speaking in council is inevitably counter-productive. First, such speaking is never forthright, truly from the heart; instead, it is grudging, distorted, partial. Second, a person who feels coerced into speaking is seldom able to listen devoutly with the heart; instead, the person is thinking what to say and how to say it, planning on how to give the minimum possible disclosure, deciding what partial or counterfeit disclosures may satisfy the group demands for community. Third, the person may not be back. The council experience was unpleasant, awkward, and embarrassing. A person who feels coerced into disclosure in council has suffered an abuse of trust and will hesitate to repeat the experience.

AFFIRMATION

Finally the participants can agree that after each participant finishes his or her turn, even if the participant says nothing, the other participants recognize the communication with an affirmation. I have been taught to use the expression *aho!* for this affirmation. This is a way of praising the courage of a speaker, including the courage of one who stays silent. Such affirmations provide immediate positive feedback for each contribution to the council. For a shy person making a first attempt at self-disclosure in council, a powerful *aho!* from the group can be a potent reinforcement.

The affirmation should be strong—loud enough to be clearly heard, not so loud as to break the flow of council. Adolescents especially may sometimes need some practice to steer a middle course between mumbling and shouting, but most circles quickly find the right level.

Different circles may choose to use different affirmations. At one circle a participant said that at his church instead of *amen* they said *amani,* the Swahili word for peace, and he asked whether, as he grew council within his church, this word might be used as an affirmation instead of *aho!* Everyone thought that was a wonderful idea. Circles can experiment, if they wish, with using affirmations such as *good!* or *thank you.*

We must bear in mind that coercion can be subtle as well as overt. In some circles I have seen the *aho!* used as an acknowledgment that the listener has been moved or touched in some way by the speaker's words or silence; in others, the *aho!* is simply an acknowledgment that the communication has been heard. My own preference is for the latter use of the affirmation: *every* communication is affirmed, whether the listener likes it or not, agrees with it or not, or was touched by it or not. I believe that every communicative act in council should be perceived as sacred; in fact, the affirmative *aho!* is a recognition that, in each communicative act, spirit is trying, however awkwardly, to make itself heard. If the *aho!* is construed as being in some sense a signal of *approval,* on the other hand, it can become—even unintentionally—covert reinforcement for a particular content or manner of speaking desired by others in the circle, and therefore coercive and hierarchical.

6
What Is Council About?

Council is never about anything in particular. It has no goal, no purpose, no agenda, no timetable. Participants could sit together in a circle for twenty minutes, silently, slowly, carefully passing the talking stick around, with no words spoken, and that might be a deeply heart-opening experience, leaving the participants mysteriously in tune, at peace with each other.

There have been a number of names used for circles called for particular purposes. People may meet in a *talking circle* just to talk—tell their stories, share their hopes and dreams, express their disappointments and regrets. People may meet in a *healing circle*—the term comes from circles called by Ojibwe elder women to confront and heal sexual abuse in their communities—to offer support to victims of harm, to share the pain of trauma or loss. People may meet in a *celebration circle* to honor a person or celebrate an accomplishment. Communities may meet in *sentencing circles*—the term was first used by the Yukon Territorial Court and has now spread to many Canadian First Nations—to create plans for offenders and victims in the criminal justice system. People may meet in *circles of understanding* in which a person who has harmed another may talk about what happened. A *reintegration circle* may be held to bring back into the community a person who has been away at war, or in prison, or on a long journey, or who had been estranged or expelled.

We should try to be very careful not to reify such names; they should be taken as description rather than prescription. Circles have their own intentions. Healing may become celebration; understanding may become reintegration. In the final analysis, council is always council, and it will go where it needs to go, whatever we may start out having called it. We must be careful not to restrict the direction just because it does not fit our agenda. We must be careful not to think that our labels are wiser than the circle.

Many times the council is called to deal with a particular topic: *We should circle up and talk about the best way to organize our fund-raiser.* Sometimes a topic for discussion will come up during the council: *I am hearing what seems to me to be a lot of anger about this. Maybe we should put that anger out front and talk about it.*

Sometimes the topic can simply be a way of loosening things up and getting things going: *Let's pass the stick around and everyone tells the most outrageous thing you would like to do.* Sometimes the topic can be a way of digging deeper into ourselves, opening up, creating bonds: *What has caused you pain in your life?* Here are a few more suggestions; I am sure you can think of others.

◇ When were you most scared?

◇ If you could bring one book to a desert island, what would it be?

◇ What are you most proud of in your life so far?

◇ What was your most embarrassing moment?

◇ If you could suddenly have the rest of the day off, what would you do?

◇ If you could have just one superpower, what would it be and why?

◇ What is the special gift you bring to this circle?

A good way to start a regularly held circle is with a *check-in*. The stick is passed, and everyone speaks briefly about where they are at the moment, what has happened in their lives since the last council, anything that might affect the quality or content of their participation. I often like to have this put in the form of a *weather report*. A participant might say: *I have been so busy at work that I haven't had enough time with my family, and that has been making me feel really stressed. But the end is in sight. I would say the skies are cloudy but clearing.* Another way of proposing a topic like this is: *Perhaps we could all tell the council one thing about ourselves that it is important for them to know right now.* Often a new topic emerges from the initial check-in or weather report.

Or again: everyone has a *special thing*—a souvenir from a trip, a gift from a grandparent, a piece of their old baby blanket, a picture of their parents. These things are often kept in a special place, deep in a closet, or in a cigar box under the bed. Here the topic is: *Bring your special thing to the next council and tell its story.* People have brought in guitars, pictures of their 1967 Ford Thunderbird convertible, photos of their pets. I have had people bring in the half-empty pack of cigarettes left when they quit smoking; one woman—an avid swimmer—brought in a bowl of water; one young man came in wearing a kilt. And all of them, often to tears and laughter, have told the wonderful stories behind their special things.

A topic can be part of an opening ceremony. A circle can be begun by participants *calling in their teachers.* All of us have in our lives people who have been our teachers, mentors, wise elders, moral guides. Such teachers and elders may still be alive, or have passed on; they do not even have to be actual people but may be characters in books. We pass the stick so that participants can name their teachers, describe them, and invite them to give us the benefit of their presence in council with us. Similarly, where participants have placed personal items on the altar, they can speak about those items, and about their history, significance, and symbolism. Or a topic may be a way to close the council: *Maybe we could each say what we are taking away from the circle today.*

Starting a circle with a given topic can serve an important learning function. Sitting in circle together is the most natural thing in the world, but we are so estranged from our deepest human roots that it has become something to be learned. I often liken council to writing a sonnet. If you want to learn to write sonnets, then you have to write *lots* of sonnets, and most of them will be pretty bad. But you are learning to master the sonnet *form,* so that, when true inspiration strikes, the sonnet form is there for you to use, like a tool ready to hand.

Council is the same way. It takes practice. A group

that wants to make council part of its life, to build council into its community, will have to sit in circle many times, and many of those council sessions will not be particularly inspired or inspiring. But when the time comes when council is truly needed, there it will be, ready to hand, a tool fashioned for use.

There is nothing wrong with any of this as long as we recognize that circle will move in its own direction. It will go where spirit—the collective wisdom, the hidden wishes, the inner dynamic of *that particular moment*—wants it to go, and that deeper motion must be recognized, honored, and not resisted.

There does not have to be a topic at all. The stick can be passed for no purpose other than for each participant to speak what is in his or her heart at that very moment. And topics themselves evolve and sometimes lurch in unexpected directions. It is easy to perceive such a change of direction as a distraction, a detour, off topic, deviating from the agenda. But remember that this is taking place in sacred time, which has no agenda. If you have asked people to circle up to talk about organizing the fund-raiser, it is easy to be frustrated when the circle starts talking about the problems of being the caretaker of an aging parent. You are frustrated because you don't see the relevance. *But it is relevant to the circle,* and it is imposing hierarchy to think that you know better than the circle what the circle is about. The fund-raiser may just have to wait; the circle knows what the circle needs *at that moment,* and that is where the circle goes.

In one circle, while calling in the teachers, one participant invited her deceased brother, who had been gay. This clearly opened a door that people had wanted to be opened; all at once everyone was talking about gay relatives and their problems; people started talking about their own sexual orientations. This is where the circle needed to go at that moment, and it went there. *At that moment* the circle opened its heart to this unexpected topic, and the result was a deeper bond and a stronger community.

PART II

❂

Applied Peacemaking

7
Stories

What do we do when we sit in council? We tell *stories*—stories of our day, stories of our hopes and fears and regrets, stories of our lives. We tell stories about the conflicts we hope to heal and the decisions we have to make. The key to peacemaking is learning to listen devoutly with our hearts to the stories of others and tell our own stories honestly from the heart in the safe and sacred space and time of the council circle. It is the goal of council—it is the *purpose* of council—for participants to feel safe enough in sacred space and time to tell their complete stories in an atmosphere of devout listening.

COMPONENTS OF STORIES

For a peacemaker, the basic unit of human communication is the *story*. It is easy to recognize that something is a story because you can give it a title—"The Tale of the Nasty Traffic Cop and the Unwarranted Speeding Ticket"; "The Story of the Clever Customer Service Representative Who Solved Our Problem"; "The Saga of the No Good Terrible Awful Day."

Every story, too, has three components—facts, feelings, and needs. The problem is that many people, most of the time, hide the last two components. Peacemaking occurs when people tell each other their stories—their *complete* stories, including what they want and what they need. Eliciting complete stories, especially from people in pain, is one of the arts of the peacemaker. Sitting in circle provides a space within which people can feel safe enough to tell their stories.

Here is an example of a story. Let's say you come home at the end of the day and tell your spouse or your roommate or your partner: *You would not believe the traffic on the expressway. It took me an hour and a half to get home.*

We know this is a story because we can give it a title—maybe something like "The Story of the Horrible Long Drive." What can we say about the story's three components?

The story is pretty clear about the facts. There was a lot of traffic on the expressway, and it took an hour and a half to get home. Most stories are pretty clear about the facts; facts are the sort of thing people are comfortable talking about. When people are in conflict, they can spend *years* arguing about who did what when—that is, arguing about the facts. Yet *facts are the least important part of the story.* The important components of the story are feelings and needs, and people do not feel comfortable talking about them.

Why should that be? The answer is simple. All of us have been taught over the years that if we talk honestly about our feelings, people will think we are wrong or bad or crazy to have those feelings. Even worse is our fear of revealing our needs. We are afraid that if we tell someone honestly what we need, people will think that we are wrong or bad or crazy for needing such a thing.

Most of us have been told things like: *There's no reason for you to be so angry. I'll talk to you when you feel better. Don't be sad. Don't make such a fuss about it. It's not worth being upset about.* In other words, if you are angry, or sad, or upset, then you are wrong, or bad, or crazy for feeling that way. When you tell "The Story of the Horrible Long Drive," you stick to the facts, because you are afraid that if you tell the listener that you are angry or frustrated or annoyed by the long drive, the listener will say, *Don't feel that way.* You are afraid that, if you tell the listener that you need a hug or a drink or ten minutes alone after the long drive, the listener will say, *What do you need that for?*

But people want and need to tell complete stories, and we, as devout listeners, have a responsibility to help them do so. We cannot make peace with another person or help two people or groups of people make peace with each other if everyone does not tell their complete stories, and speak honestly about their feelings and needs.

THE FOUR TOOLS

People tell complete stories when they feel safe. We—and the circles within which we sit—have four tools we can use to help people tell their complete stories to us or to another person. We will call these tools *listening, reflecting, exploring,* and *validating.*

Listening

The primary, most basic, and most powerful tool we have is simply devout listening. I would guess that 80 percent of the time devout listening is enough to make the storyteller feel safe enough to tell a complete story.

A participant in one of my workshops told me this story. Her husband had recently become filled with anger, which focused on the upcoming wedding of their daughter. He was constantly yelling and complaining about the young man, the cost of the wedding, the young man's parents; he was becoming hard to live with. She, of course, had said all the things people say in that situation: *I don't understand what you're so angry about. There's no need to be so upset. Come on, you're spoiling the wedding.* In other words, she had been telling him that he was wrong or bad or crazy for feeling what he was feeling.

So she decided to try listening—to create a safe space, a *sacred* space, where her husband could think through his feelings and his needs. She would hold that space for him, listening devoutly, not speaking or responding, for as long as it took. And here is what he said:

> *This @!$%*! wedding! We're going to be in the poorhouse before it's over. And that guy! What a jerk! He'll never amount to anything. Just like his parents! Cheapskates! They haven't even volunteered to pay for the liquor . . .*

This went on for a while. Then he said:

> *I don't know why I'm so upset all the time. This really isn't like me. I just get so angry. Well, not even angry. Upset, like I'm losing something. I feel like I'm losing my daughter. And that just makes me feel so helpless . . .*

Then, after a while, he said:

> *I guess that's what's going on. I love her so much. We've always had this very special relationship. Now I'm afraid all that will change. I'm losing my little girl. She'll have her own family, and she won't need me anymore.*

Finally he said:

> *I guess I should go speak with her, tell her I'm sorry for being such a jerk. I should tell her that I'll always love her, that I'll always be her dad. I guess that's what I'll do.*

Reflecting

Another powerful tool is to *reflect* an unspoken part of the story: *Boy, from what you're telling me it sounds like that made you pretty mad. From the way you're talking about it, you seem to be fed up with the whole situation. When I see the way you're sitting there, you look really sad about that.*

There are generally two parts to a good reflection. First, it should be grounded in an observation of the storyteller's behavior: *From what you've said . . . From the way you're pacing back and forth . . . When I see you sitting there like that . . .* Second, it should be clearly labeled as a reflection: *It sounds like . . . It seems that . . . I guess that . . . It looks to me like . . .* A good listener does not have to pretend to be a mind reader. A good listener makes reasonable reflections based on observable behavior. Still, a natural-sounding reflection can be compressed: *You seem really upset.*

One of the powerful things about reflecting is that

you do not have to be right. Reflecting works just as well if you're wrong. In fact, sometimes it works even *better* when you're wrong. Suppose the listener says to the teller of "The Story of the Horrible Long Drive," *Boy, from the way you talk about that, you seem to be pretty angry.* The storyteller can say the reflection is right: *Well, no kidding, of course I'm angry.* The storyteller can say the reflection is wrong: *No, I'm not angry so much as I'm just frustrated.* In either case, we are no longer talking about the facts. We are now talking about feelings, and that was the goal of the reflecting—to help the storyteller tell a complete story, including feelings.

The same principles hold true for reflecting what the storyteller needs. People are even more reluctant to talk about their needs than they are to talk about their feelings, and a reflection gives them permission and safety: *My guess is you might need a few minutes to unwind. I bet you could use a drink.* Then the storyteller can say: *Actually, I need a hug.* Or often: *I just need to vent; I'm glad you're listening.*

Exploring

Reflecting is, essentially, making an inference about an unspoken part of a story. *Exploring*, on the other hand, is straight-out asking questions about it: *How did you feel about that? What was going on with that? Can you give me an example?* Exploring does not necessarily have to be in question form—for example, *I noticed that you hesitated right there; I wonder if that was something important to you.* You can ask about needs as well as about feelings: *Would you like a few minutes by yourself? How about a hug?* In fact, you can ask in the most straightforward possible way: *What do you need? How can I help?* And there is the one all-purpose way to ask for more information: *Tell me more about that.*

Bear in mind that you are exploring, not giving advice; the goal is to *evoke discernment,* not impose a solution that seems right to you. That is why, in exploring, we only ask questions; we do not make statements or suggestions. And the questions should not be disguised advice or rhetorical questions: *Why don't you try meditating? Have you thought of seeing a therapist?* Just as in council, there is no fixing, no saving, no advising, no setting straight. The questions must be authentic, challenging, caring, open, brief, unhurried, and asked out of genuine interest and sympathetic curiosity. The person exploring can pause after each answer, making sure that the speaker is finished, providing space for further thinking.

The sorts of questions that can be used in exploring can go directly to eliciting a complete story: *How do you feel about that? What do you need to make this right?* They can be about the feelings and needs of other people involved, the storyteller's fears and concerns, whether it is time to take action, whether the storyteller feels a sense of obligation or resentment or fear of disapproval—all motivated by genuine interest in what the storyteller has to say.

In his book *A Hidden Wholeness,* Parker Palmer, a Quaker educator and peace activist, uses the terms *honest* and *open* to characterize such genuinely exploratory questions. An *honest* question, he writes, is one to which the questioner cannot imagine what the right answer might be; an *open* question is one that does not frame the situation in order to suggest the answer—a question that "expands rather than restricts your arena of exploration." Honest and open questions—*When you say you are frustrated, what do you mean?*—welcome the soul to speak its truth. But questions such as *Didn't that make you angry?* or *Why are you so sad?* are, despite any good intentions, neither honest nor open. They suggest that the questioner already knows the right response; they constrict the listener's ability to respond. And in their presumption, Palmer says, they scare away the listener's soul.

And remember that *silence is always acceptable.* Be patient with the storyteller's silence, and with your own. If you can't think of a question, perhaps silence is what is needed *at that moment.*

Validating

Finally, a fourth way to help someone tell a complete story is to *validate* the story—that is, reassure the storyteller that you do not in fact think it is wrong or bad or crazy to feel or need what the storyteller feels or needs: *I guess most people would feel that way. Probably just about anyone would be angry in that situation. I think it's perfectly natural to feel sad about that kind of setback.* You can validate needs: *After an hour and a half in traffic, I bet just about anyone would need time to unwind.* Or again, there is one single all-purpose way to validate a story: *I can understand that.*

COMBINING THE TOOLS

Splitting things up this way can make reflecting, exploring, and validating seem awkward and unnatural. And yet they are the most natural things in the world. It is the way we naturally respond when we are interested and curious and compassionate and helpful—that is, when we are really listening devoutly. Inferring, asking, and validating can also be combined in all sorts of ways: *You seem really angry. What can I do to help?*

Try this little exercise with one other person. I call it the *blessing exercise,* because it involves stating your highest and best hopes for another person's life, and that person stating the same to you. Ask this person to tell you about a time he or she felt safe, nurtured, secure, supported, taken care of—when the person felt held, protected in the arms of the universe. This could be a memory from childhood or an experience with a loved one or an incident on a trip or at work or in the wilderness. Hand that person your talking stick, and listen devoutly with your heart. Listening may be enough; but feel free, as you are moved to do so, to reflect, explore, and validate. Create a sacred space and time within which that person feels safe enough, understood enough, and unrushed enough to tell the complete story of that experience.

Then, take back the stick and, based on the complete story you heard, *bless* the person who spoke to you; that is, tell the person your highest and best hopes and wishes for that person's life, using as your basis the person's own story. Begin with the words *May you . . .* and proceed from there. Be poetic; use the person's story as a metaphor. Close with *May it be so.* Then you and the other person can change places.

You can apply these tools when sitting in council. When the stick reaches you, you can say: *It seems to me that Richard is really upset about this situation. I'm hoping that he will tell us more about how he feels.* Or: *I would like to ask Richard whether this is something he really wants to do or if he is just going along with the rest of us.* Or: *I can understand why Richard is so upset about this.*

And, of course, in council we can all *tell* our complete stories. We can say: *I'm feeling a little nervous because we seem to be moving too fast on this. I need a little time to think this through.* Or: *I'm feeling frustrated at the way our position was ignored by the program committee. I need to figure out a way they will give it full consideration.*

8
Advice

When people are in conflict, or are troubled, or have been involved in a harm, they often say they want advice. In part, this is a reflection of the loss of self-efficacy which is a natural part of the decentering response to conflict. It is also embedded within a hierarchical culture that assumes that some people are wiser, better, or more moral than other people, and therefore know what is best for other people, and are in a position to tell other people what to do.

In our transactional culture, too, when people come to you for advice, when they subordinate themselves to your wisdom or morality, it is considered inappropriate to withhold your part of the transaction. It goes against our hierarchical and transactional culture to keep from solving other people's problems, and instead to create a sacred space within which people can discern their own needs.

I am not talking about what we can call *technical* advice. If my car or computer is not working properly, there are people with technical expertise who can tell me how to get it running again. If I am having trouble setting up a wireless network, there are people who can help me with that. But there are limits to technical advice. If I am weighing the purchase of a camera that is inexpensive but has few features against a camera that is more expensive and has more features, then someone who knows a lot about cameras may be able to tell me what the various features do; but only I can determine which balance of cost and features is best for *me*.

If we really believe that people are autonomous self-healing problem solvers, then we have to believe that they *do not need advice*. They may need listening, reflecting, exploring, and validation; they certainly need a chance to be heard, to tell their story, to have a sacred space within which they can think through for themselves what they really need.

This idea goes against all of our hierarchical conditioning. This is because giving advice *creates hierarchy*. It creates a space within which one person is a supplicant, and the other is an expert. We want to give advice because we get tired of listening. We want to give advice because we think we are smarter, or wiser, or better than the other person. We want to give advice because we are focused on outcomes, solutions, fixing things. We want to give advice because we view the interaction transactionally: *Give me your subordination, and I will solve your problem.* When we think transactionally, we are even uncomfortable *not* giving advice, because we think we *owe* advice in return for a story.

I know this sounds harsh. Surely we give advice out of love, compassion, a desire to help. But instead of giving advice, a peacemaker just listens devoutly. If the other person seems to be demanding to be given advice, we can put that issue out front by reflecting: *I think I hear you saying that you want me to make this decision for you.* The same is true in council. Participants can reflect and explore and validate: *It seems to me that Mary is having trouble reaching a decision, and she wants the circle to make the decision for her. I am wondering whether John feels he is being pressured to come to a conclusion on this.*

The next time you are listening to someone and you feel the urge to give advice, look for a moment at what is going on inside your own head. I would guess that it is something like this: *How long have we been talking here? I can't sit here any longer. We're not getting anywhere. What a bad idea! I know just what will work. This is taking too long.* Of course, while such thoughts are going through your head, you are not listening.

When people ask for advice, a peacemaker can say quite honestly: I do not know what someone else should do. I do not know what anyone else needs, or what is best for someone else. My ability to tell the future is severely limited. I do not know where you are on your journey. All I know how to do is create a sacred space of listening in which you can speak with your own best self. *Come. Sit down. Let's talk.*

During John Paul Lederach's training on peacebuilding in protracted interethnic conflict, one of the participants asked him how he knew when the two sides he had brought together were getting close to a resolution. He said he never knew when they were getting closer, because he had no idea where they were going. He said he had no idea what the best solution was *for them*. Something that seemed like a good solution to him might not be what they needed; what they needed might meet none of his expectations. He could only hold the space for them while they worked it out for themselves.

9
Conflict

THE NATURE OF CONFLICT

Often, when I talk to students about peacemaking, I write the word *conflict* on the board and ask the class to shout out the first words that come to mind when they think about conflict. You will not be surprised to learn that most of the words they say are negative: *argument, fighting, war, anger, loss, threat.* It takes a lot of coaxing to come up with some positive associations: *resolution, understanding, learning, voice, creativity.*

Conflict has a bad reputation.

That is why we hear terms such as *conflict resolution* and *conflict management.* Conflict is supposed to be bad, and therefore it must be controlled, ended, put away, *managed, resolved.* But I would like to propose two rules of conflict that go against this common perception:

- ◇ Conflict is inevitable.
- ◇ Conflict is good.

There is, after all, no avoiding conflict. No two people, much less two groups of people, agree on everything. People differ in their goals and in their ways of trying to reach their goals. You can't hide from conflict, and you can't pretend it doesn't exist. At the same time, conflict presents an opportunity to deepen relationships, strengthen community, and increase connection.

Here is an exercise I always enjoy doing with my classes. I divide them into pairs, and tell each pair to pretend that they are coworkers who are planning to have a nice dinner out together on a Friday evening after a long stressful work week. But number one in each pair wants Mexican food, craves Mexican food, has been *dreaming* about Mexican food; while number two had Mexican food last weekend, and now is really craving Thai food.

A conflict! Mexican food against Thai food! Argument, fighting, war, anger! I tell the class they have two minutes to deal with the conflict. And they do.

People come up with wonderful solutions. They agree to go to a food court, so both can have the food they want. They agree to go to a Mexican restaurant for appetizers and margaritas and then to a Thai restaurant for dinner. They agree to try a third kind of food, such as Ethiopian, that neither has ever had before. They agree to go shopping for ingredients and cook at one of their homes. One pair decided they would try to make enchiladas with peanut sauce.

I think there are two lessons to be learned from this little exercise. First, people come up with these wonderful solutions because, when I tell them that there is a conflict between Mexican and Thai food, *they do not believe me.* They quickly and easily reframe the apparent conflict into a *mutual unmet need*—that is, a mutual unmet need to have a pleasant evening together. Once the apparent conflict has been reframed into this mutual unmet need, the solutions appear as if by magic.

Second, *the solution does not matter.* People enjoy this exercise because it deepens relationships. The people in the class, who are often strangers to each other, feel just a little closer to the other person in the pair, because they have shared the experience of working together to meet a mutual unmet need. The process is infinitely more valuable than the product.

It is surprising how often people think they are in conflict when they are not. When we have an unmet need, we often look around to find a person to blame. We tend to believe that an unmet need is another person's fault, and of course, in our culture our first impulse is to identify and then punish that person.

Actually, the repertoire of human needs is relatively limited. We all need respect, safety, appreciation, information, fairness, justice, a chance to be heard. We all need to be regarded as a good and worthwhile person, to have some degree of control over our lives, and to believe that we are doing the right thing. Buddhist peace activist Thich Nhat Hanh says that one role of the peacemaker is simply to bring the pain of each side to the attention of the other. Here is a mutual unmet need in its rawest form—the need for everyone to give voice to his or her pain.

A conflict is about unmet needs. Peacemaking in a situation of apparent conflict involves reframing the conflict so that the participants can see the mutual unmet needs they share. That is why it is so important for the peacemaker to tell a complete story and to encourage everyone else to do the same. The parties to an apparent conflict cannot recognize that their unmet needs are mutual unless they feel safe enough to articulate what they need. And often all it takes is listening. As peacemaker Christopher Titmuss said about his Israeli-Palestinian workshops: "Listening, without any particular intention to resolve the conflict, seems to bring its own insight. There is a great, great need to be heard and feel understood."

APPROACHING CONFLICT

Why then does conflict have such a bad reputation? I think it is because finding yourself suddenly in conflict produces a disconcerting psychological response, which we can think of as a sort of *dislocation* or *decentering*. This natural response has two aspects. First, suddenly finding yourself in an apparent conflict takes away your self-efficacy. You feel confused, uncertain, indecisive, powerless, dependent. And second, it makes you self-protective. You become hypervigilant, hostile, suspicious, closed-minded; you begin to develop a victim-oppressor narrative, and you start to dehumanize and demonize the other person.

Let's say you are stopped at a stop sign, and suddenly someone comes up too quickly behind you and hits your car in the rear end. There you were, happy, carefree, in your beautiful car, and now, all at once, you are jerked from your calm and steady state, dislocated, off center: *My car! Is my car okay? Is my insurance up to date? What do I do? Do I call the police? Am I all right? Do I have whiplash?*

Even more, you turn your dismay into demonizing the other driver. *That idiot! Where did he buy his license? And look at that horrible car he's driving. What a moron!* And what do you think—go ahead, admit it—if the driver is a member of a different racial or ethnic group: *Those damn —s! They never could drive. Probably stoned.*

Now, this psychological reaction is perfectly natural. It probably goes back a long way. *Whoa! Goddamn saber-tooth tiger!* And then: *Those damn animals! We need to hunt them all down!* along with a big surge of helpful fight-or-flight adrenaline.

But nowadays, under most circumstances, the reaction is largely dysfunctional. Even worse, this acute psychological reaction can become chronic. So how do we deal with conflict?

One approach to conflict is *transactional:* you give up this, and I will give up that, and although we are both dissatisfied, the conflict will go away. The transactional assumption is that conflicts are zero sum—that a gain to one person is inevitably a loss to the other. Lawyers sometimes say that a settlement is a good one if everyone walks away unhappy; this is the essential transactional view.

The other approach is *transformational:* see conflict as an opportunity to deepen relations. Try this exercise. Sit down with a friend and an orange and figure out how to share the whole orange. It is not a solution to cut the orange in half, because then each of you gets only half an orange. The solution cannot be a compromise, where each one gives up part of the orange; the solution has to be one in which you both get the benefit of the whole orange.

Here are some solutions people in my classes have come up with. Take the seeds from the orange and plant them together in flowerpots, to grow orange trees. Stud the orange with whole cloves, and hang it in the kitchen as an air freshener. Grate the orange peel and squeeze the orange juice to make orange muffins together.

What all of these solutions have in common is that they involve activity together: *the joint activity becomes more important than the orange.* Planting seeds together, making muffins together; these—and not written agreements, compromise, and settlement—are the way to peace.

MEDIATION AND PEACEMAKING

Many court systems have instituted a formal program of mediation for certain types of civil actions—personal injury litigation, complex contract cases, product and professional liability actions, commercial litigation. Private mediation of such disputes is considered particularly suitable where the parties want to preserve an ongoing relationship, where highly confidential or proprietary information is involved, or where a quick resolution would avoid serious economic disruption.

Lawyers certified as mediators sit down with the parties to the dispute, try to narrow their areas of disagreement, keep the discussion on track, suggest compromises, and guide the parties toward an agreement that is formalized in a memorandum submitted to the court. Sometimes the mediator may caucus separately with one or the other of the parties, again in order to open up areas of compromise and agreement. These mediation sessions usually last anywhere from a few hours to a full day. Mediators are paid by the parties, and the mediators are rated based on the percentage of their cases that produce a memorandum of agreement.

Such mediation is considered an efficient way to keep disputes out of court. And there is much justice that is done by such mediation, especially in comparison to cases that go to full-blown litigation. But it is not *sacred* justice.

Such mediations are deeply embedded in our cultural system, and thus they are inherently hierarchical and transactional. The goal is not a deeper relationship between the parties, but rather a formal agreement that is considered a contract by the court. Professional mediators are motivated by the rating system to produce an agreement, and they encourage the parties to behave transactionally—to compromise, to give something to get something, to lose this point in order to win that point. And the mediators are figures of authority, trained and certified by the court, who are supposed to guide the discussion, avoid what they consider irrelevancies, suggest what they consider the most viable solutions, and assist in drafting the formal agreement.

Peacemaking, in comparison, can seem slow, inefficient, inconclusive. The peacemaker sits down with the parties in a council circle; helps the parties to create a sacred space and time within which they can speak honestly and listen devoutly; passes the talking stick; models by showing how to listen devoutly; gives no advice, suggests no compromises, urges no outcomes, and lets the circle go where it wants; and aims only to let the parties tell their complete stories to each other. The goal is for the peacemaker to hold a space within which the parties, as autonomous self-healing problem solvers, can identify their own mutual unmet needs and, in the process, deepen their relationship and learn to walk in peace with each other.

I should add that there is nothing *wrong* with an agreement, even a written one, if it is an outcome the parties come to on their own. They may agree verbally that they will make orange muffins together; they may agree, in writing, to a detailed timeline for actions they promise to take. But the process does not *aim* at such agreements; they arise instead spontaneously out of the process itself.

Thus, whether the parties are two neighbors in a dispute over a property line or two ethnic groups who have engaged in bloody conflict for generations, the peacemaking process engages what John Paul Lederach calls the parties' *moral imagination*. Seemingly miraculously, out of the deeply human need to be in right relationship, the parties find themselves coming together. The process might take weeks or years, or there might be a sudden unexpected breakthrough to mutual understanding. But the process is paramount—egalitarian, liberating, and transformational.

10
Dealing with Anger

THE NATURE OF ANGER

One of the problems in being a peacemaker is that many of us are afraid of anger: both our own anger and the anger of other people. Because we are afraid of our own anger, we avoid situations in which we might become angry; because we are afraid of other people's anger, we avoid or reject an angry person. But a peacemaker is not afraid of anger. A peacemaker recognizes two truths about anger:

◇ All anger has a life-serving core.
◇ All anger is a response to an unmet need.

These two truths mean that people who are angry believe that they are being denied something they need in order to live—respect, safety, information, fairness, justice, a chance to be heard. Most frequently, people are angry because they believe that no one is listening to them. And in our culture they are often right.

If these two statements are true, then what's wrong with being angry? I think there are two problems. First, anger can be addictive. It is a rush; it gives us a sense of power; its *purpose,* deep down in our lizard brains, is to give us the strength to meet our unmet needs. That's potent stuff, and many people come to love the feeling.

Second, anger can—rather like alcohol—be a great deceiver. Anger can make you think that you are being powerful and commanding, when in fact it is making you act like a jerk. We've all seen it—the angry man whose flight has been canceled, yelling at the gate agent at the podium: *What's wrong with you people?* Only people in the grip of anger would yell at someone who has no power to alter the situation but does have the ability to have the angry person's luggage sent to Afghanistan.

Some people have great difficulty knowing what they need. They have been taught to hide their needs even from themselves. Sometimes it is important for a peacemaker to listen devoutly to the unspoken story that is told by behavior rather than by speech. This can be difficult when the behavior is aggressive or threatening, but it is worth the effort.

For example, suppose John is angry and yelling. He is actually pretty scary because it is not clear whether he will spin out of control. It is worth asking: *Why is he yelling?* Most of the time the answer is that he is yelling because he believes that no one will listen to him unless he yells. And the reason he believes that is because it is what he has been taught, and because it is often true. The same thing is true if John is threatening or trying to bully other people: *I'll call my lawyer! I'll get you fired!*

But a peacemaker knows that both John and the peace-maker have a mutual unmet need for John to be listened to, and for John to feel safe enough to tell a complete story. So the peacemaker meets anger and threats and bullying with the magic words: *Come. Sit down. Let's talk.*

DEALING WITH THE ANGER OF OTHERS

A parent barges into the school principal's office, yelling: *My son has a bloody knee! He says he got pushed on the playground. What is wrong with you people?*

The principal suddenly finds herself in an apparent conflict. She is taken aback, decentered, perhaps getting an adrenaline jolt of her own. So it is understandable that the principal may be tempted to handle this situation in a way that increases conflict rather than makes peace and mends the relationship.

And there are lots of wrong ways to handle this interaction. The principal may be tempted to turn it into an argument about the facts: *Hmm, are you sure it happened here?* Or the principal could tell the angry parent that he is wrong or bad or crazy to be angry: *I'm sorry, sir. I can't talk with you when you are so angry.*

But neither of these approaches lessens the anger, opens dialogue, or helps to heal a broken relationship of trust.

So let's take a minute and do some inferring. What is this yelling parent feeling? A good guess is that he is angry. He is probably also frustrated, worried about his child, and concerned about whether he has made a good choice of school.

But mostly, right at this moment, he is angry. And this in turn means that he has needs that are not being met.

So what does this yelling parent need? A good guess is that he needs some reassurance that his child is safe. He probably needs to know that he is a good parent who has not made a mistake sending his child to this school. He probably needs to understand how the accident could have happened. He needs his trust in the school restored. But mostly, right at this moment, he needs to be heard.

So the principal says the magic words: *Come. Sit down. Tell me about this.* And then the principal does two things. First, she creates a space within which the angry parent can tell a complete story. She listens devoutly, providing the sacred space and time within which the parent can come around to his feelings and needs. When necessary, she reflects, explores, and validates: *I can see that you are really upset about this. I can certainly understand that. If my son had been hurt on the playground, I'd be pretty upset about it too. I would guess that you need to know that your son is safe in our school. How can we approach dealing with that?*

Notice how the principal is reframing the apparent conflict into mutual unmet needs, because the principal and the parent *really need exactly the same things.* They both need to know that the school is a safe place for the child, and that the parent made a good decision in sending the child to the school. It is just like the apparent conflict between Thai and Mexican food. The search for *who to blame,* whose fault it was, is a distraction from finding their mutual unmet need to make sure the school is as safe as possible.

Once that has been accomplished, the parent's anger

has vanished. The principal and the parent are now *working together* to meet their mutual unmet needs. They are planting orange trees; they are making orange muffins together. The principal can explain the existing rules, and explain the delicate balance between risk and autonomy on the playground. She can ask for suggestions on how to improve the process. Maybe they can talk about getting parent volunteers to come assist in monitoring activity on the playground; maybe they can consider changes to playground equipment. But as always, *solutions are not important*. It is the working together that creates the community, deepens their relationship, and repairs the bonds of trust.

DEALING WITH YOUR OWN ANGER

A peacemaker is human and sometimes gets angry. But a peacemaker immediately recognizes the anger for what it is—a *messenger* who bears the message that the peacemaker has an unmet need. Unless the unmet need is, say, the need to escape a charging mastodon, there is no reason to keep the anger around once it has delivered its message. The important thing is to figure out what the unmet need is, and the best way to meet it; and anger—with its yelling, threats, and bluster—is usually not the best way to respond.

So it is often best just to *thank the messenger* and send it on its way and try to puzzle out the message. And I mean: thank the messenger. Think to yourself, or even say out loud, if no one can hear you: *Thank you, anger. I really appreciate your pointing out to me that I have an unmet need.*

You have done your job. Please go, with my gratitude. I'll take it from here.

Sometimes the anger does not want to go; perhaps you are really enjoying the sense of self-righteous power that anger is giving you. The anger will tell you: *You need me. Only I can get you what you need. Without me, no one will listen to you.* But there are two things you know about anger:

◇ Anger demands action.

◇ Anger feeds on itself.

Because anger demands action, one thing you can do when you are angry is to *take no action*. Wait. Count to ten. Think of something else. Think of something pleasant. Let the angry moment pass.

Anger feeds on itself in two ways. First, it creates *physical tension*. You breathe more quickly, your muscles tighten, your body prepares itself to attack or flee, and in turn, you read these physical sensations as anger. Anger in the body feeds anger in the mind.

There are several ways to break this tension feedback cycle. Since anger makes you breathe fast, a good way to help the anger fade away is just to *breathe slower*. Here is a way that I have found particularly effective, but it takes a bit of preparation ahead of time. Sit comfortably, close your eyes, and picture yourself in an airport, going to meet someone you love—a good friend, a spouse, a grandchild. You are walking through the corridor, on the way to the luggage area. Use all your senses. Look at the people, the luggage carts, the signs; smell the airport air; feel the floor of the corridor against your feet; hear the flight announcements, the buzz of the crowd, the hum of the ventilating system. The plane has arrived; you scan the crowd, looking, feeling a little anxious. There she is! Running toward you, calling your name, arms open; a huge goofy, happy smile breaks out on your face.

Stop right there. Get the kinesthetic sense of that smile. Memorize what that smile feels like. Now, the next time you are angry, bring back the kinesthetic memory of that smile— not the smile itself, but what it *feels like* to have that smile. I guarantee that you cannot be angry at the same time that you are feeling that smile.

Second, anger *justifies itself.* Have you ever seen a small child throw a tantrum? At first there is a lot of energy—loud crying, arms and legs pumping, rolling around on the ground. Then the energy starts to wane, physical activity diminishes, the tears stop flowing, and the child seems to think: *What was I angry about? Oh yes.* And the second round begins.

We all do that. When our anger starts its natural decline, we pump it back up. *What was I angry about? Oh yes.* We remind ourselves why we are angry; we remember the object of our anger; we remind ourselves of how we have been wronged; we seek to recover the powerful high of our self-righteousness. Most of all, we are afraid that if we let our anger just naturally fade away, we were somehow not justified in being angry in the first place. So we keep it going.

A way to break both the bodily and mental tension feedback cycle is through mindfulness. Relax, step back, and simply observe the state of your body; note the areas that are tense, observe the breath going in and out, perceive kinesthetically how your body is positioned in space. In the same way, simply watch the thoughts going through your mind: *How dare he do that? That was so rude and stupid. What a jerk.* Do not get caught up in the thoughts; just watch them drift through your mind, like leaves on a stream. As you step back and observe the state of your body and mind with bare attention—even a sort of wry detachment—you will find that you are calming down, your bodily tension is dissolving, and the angry thoughts begin to be just thoughts, transient and ineffectual.

11
Harms

NEEDS IN SITUATIONS OF HARM

Peacemaking is a way of meeting together, making decisions, solving problems, dealing with conflicts, and building community. Among these decisions, problems, conflicts, and threats to community, the most poignant and wrenching are those that involve the harm that people do to each other. And of course, every conflict involves some perceived harm—an injustice, a betrayal, an invasion, a deprivation.

People harm each other in many different ways. People may be harmed by being physically injured, sexually abused, manipulated, threatened, verbally abused, publicly shamed, treated like an object, rejected, betrayed, violated, overlooked, taken for granted, falsely accused, treated unfairly, reduced in status, denied a voice, dehumanized, denigrated for their beliefs, or deprived of basic social goods, such as education, employment, housing, or freedom.

Now that you have read this list, I would like you to take a moment and do two things. First, recall *the worst harm you have ever suffered from another person.* This may be painful. Think about how you felt at the time, and how you feel about it now. Think about your needs now in relation to what happened and the person who did it to you. Think about what you would say if you were sitting in council right now, telling a complete story of this harm to the other person.

Let me try guessing some of your thoughts. I would guess that at the time of the harm—and perhaps even now—you felt angry, humiliated, ashamed, betrayed, confused, sad, isolated, helpless, damaged, and alone. I would guess that at the time of the harm—and perhaps even now—your first, most basic, primary need was *to be heard,* to tell your story in a setting of safety and receptivity to people who had opened their hearts to hear you. And I would guess you had other important needs as well:

◈ To have your self-respect and dignity restored
◈ To know that the harm was not your fault
◈ To have your community recognize that you have been harmed
◈ To tell the person who harmed you the impact of the harm
◈ For the person who harmed you to be accountable for the harm
◈ To be assured that the harm will not be repeated
◈ For the harm to be repaired and things made right

Second, after you have thought about this for a while, recall *the worst harm you have ever done to another person.* This also may be painful. Think about why you did it and how you justified it to yourself at the time. Think about how you feel about it now. Think about your needs now in relation to what you did and the person you did it to. Think about what you would say if you were sitting in council right now, telling a complete story of this harm to the other person.

Again, let me try guessing some of your thoughts. As you recalled the harm that you did, I would guess that you felt embarrassed, uncomfortable, ashamed, guilty, stupid, remorseful, and apologetic. I would guess that, as you recalled the harm that you did, your first, most basic, primary need was *to be heard,* to tell your story in a setting of safety and receptivity to people who had opened their hearts to hear you. And I would guess you had other important needs as well:

- ◇ To have your self-respect and dignity restored
- ◇ To have your remorse accepted as genuine
- ◇ To not be considered a bad person
- ◇ To be safe from retaliation
- ◇ To have the opportunity to make things right
- ◇ To restore your injured relationships
- ◇ To rejoin your community

I think there are two lessons that can be learned from this experiment. First, *there are no good guys and bad guys.* Everyone has been harmed by someone; everyone has harmed someone else. Even in a single situation where a harm has been done, it can be difficult to disentangle good guys from bad guys. Everyone has a story to tell.

Second, both the harmer and the person harmed have *mutual unmet needs.* They both need to have their self-respect and dignity restored; they both need to repair the broken relationship and mend the breach of trust; they both need to see that things are made right; they both need assurances of safety—on the one hand, that the harm will not be repeated and, on the other, that there will not be revenge or retaliation for the harm. They both need to foreclose an ongoing cycle of violence.

But most of all, they both *need to be heard.* This applies to every conflict, from a schoolyard fight to multigenerational interethnic warfare. Mennonite peacemaker John Paul Lederach says that a Tajik warlord once told him, "You have to circle into the truth through stories." Those in conflict need to sit in sacred space and time, speak honestly to the other from their hearts, and listen devoutly with their hearts to the complete stories of the other.

THE COMMUNITY STAKE

We have been speaking as if there were only two participants in a situation of harm—the person who does the harm and the person who suffers the harm. But we have left out a participant of equal importance—*the community within which the harm occurred.* Every harm takes place in a community context. Let's take a simple example. During an escalating dispute in the school playground Johnny hits Timmy in the face and knocks him to the ground.

This interaction affects a much larger community than just Johnny and Timmy. It affects the other children in the school yard, who may no longer feel safe playing there. It affects the teachers who are supposed to be supervising the children in the school yard. As word spreads, it affects other children in the school. In turn, this affects the classroom teachers and then, in turn, the school administration. It affects Johnny's parents and Timmy's parents. It affects other parents, who worry about their children's safety. It affects the principal, the local school council, the parent-teacher association. It affects everyone. It affects the entire community.

In every case where one person harms another, there is community involvement. Nothing ever happens in isolation from a community context. Jonathon robs Timothy at gunpoint on a dark street in order to get money for the drugs to which he is addicted. This is not an insular event. Just as with the punch in the schoolyard, the act of harm affects everyone who hears about it. But there is more. The harm implicates a surprising number of questions including—but certainly not limited to—why the street was poorly lit, what the community can do about drug addiction, how Jonathon got possession of the gun, and whether long prison sentences for drug possession make such crimes more or less likely to happen.

I certainly do not want the issues here *reduced* to community issues. In order to repair this harm, both Jonathon and Timothy have complete stories that they need to tell each other. I would suggest here a heuristic principle: without neglecting individuals and their accountability, always look for ways in which the *community* was involved in the harm and the ways in which the community can help to repair it. As John Paul Lederach puts it: think in terms of long-term solutions; always project solutions into the future.

The community has its own unmet needs, beginning, of course, with the community's own need to be heard, to be allowed to speak honestly through its representatives in sacred space and time. And the community also needs

◇ To be safe from harm
◇ To have the harm done to the community acknowledged
◇ To mend broken relationships
◇ To affirm the community's values
◇ To reintegrate the people involved in the harm into the community

In other words, the community has its own unmet needs that overlap with the needs of everyone else.

THE PUNITIVE RESPONSE TO HARM

There are two different ways of responding to harms—by punishment and by peacemaking. There is no doubt that the overwhelmingly preferred way of dealing with harms in our culture is by punishment. The punitive response to harm asks three questions.

◇ Who broke the rule?
◇ What rule was broken?
◇ How do we punish the person who broke the rule?

If you stop and think about this for a moment, it is easy to see how pervasive this response to harm is in our culture. From raising children to judging criminals, in classrooms

and courtrooms, we are constantly asking these three questions. The focus is on *rules*—which one was broken and who
broke it; and the outcome is that the person who is declared
the rule breaker is stigmatized, punished, and given, we say
to ourselves, just what that person deserves.

Let's go back to Johnny punching Timmy on the school
playground. In our culture, we generally take this as a single
interaction between Johnny and Timmy. We are interested
in the facts of this particular case; indeed, we are obsessed
with them: *Who started it? Who hit whom?* Once we decide
that Johnny is the offender and Timmy is the victim—that
Johnny is the one who broke the rule against hitting—the
only question is how he should be punished. If we can't sat-
isfactorily decide which one of the two is the rule breaker,
we often just throw up our hands and punish them both.

Especially in schools, we often try to disguise the fact
that we are talking about punishment by using the word
consequences. But punishment is in no way a natural consequence of harming someone, in the way that, say, getting
wet is a natural consequence of standing out in the rain.
Punishment is a consequence only in the sense that our
culture has decided that it is. Every schoolchild knows that
consequence means punishment, and we only look foolish
pretending otherwise.

What is most striking about this response to harm,
however, is that it completely fails to meet the needs of any
of the stakeholders. No one gets to tell a complete story, to
be heard, to be safe, for the harm to be made right, for the
relationship between Johnny and Timmy and their community to be healed.

THE PEACEMAKING
RESPONSE TO HARM

As opposed to the punitive response to harms, there is a *peacemaking* response, consisting of

◈ Responsibility
◈ Repair
◈ Reintegration

These are worth elaborating one at a time.

Responsibility

When we speak of *accepting responsibility* for a harm, we mean that *everyone* involved in a harm has to be accountable. Most harms occur in the context of ongoing relationships, continuing interactions, and enduring communities. In these contexts, it is futile to try to *punctuate* interactions, to determine—as we are so fond of doing—who started it, who is at fault, and thus, we believe, who deserves to be punished. But as we know, such facts are the least important part of the stories. In the peacemaking approach, everyone is accountable for his or her part in what happened, and everyone accepts the responsibility to heal the broken relationships. In such contexts, there is no offender and no victim, only participants.

Here is a true story. In a high school in Chicago, a senior—a popular football player, who had been offered a college football scholarship—was dating a junior, the captain of the cheerleading squad. While standing in line at the high school cafeteria, the girl was approached by a freshman boy—apparently lacking in social skills—who kept annoying her and would not leave her alone when she asked him. Finally, the girl said to her boyfriend, "Will you make him shut up?" Whereupon the senior slapped the freshman in the face.

Unfortunately for everyone involved, someone in the cafeteria had recorded the incident on a cell phone, and the video, along with the name of the high school, was posted on YouTube. The mother of the freshman boy saw the video and complained to the school principal; the principal, invoking the school's zero-tolerance policies, reported the incident to the police; and the next day the police came to the school and arrested both the senior boy and the junior girl, taking them out of the school in handcuffs.

As a result, the boy and girl received ten-day suspensions, the senior boy lost his football scholarship, and the freshman boy was so afraid of retaliation that he stopped coming to school and eventually transferred elsewhere.

I see no way to label victims and offenders in this situation. Who was the victim in this cascade? Who was the offender? The freshman? The football player? The girl? The school principal? The zero-tolerance policy? The police? A culture that sees the criminal justice system as a way of dealing with conflict among high school students?

Where there has been a harm done, there is, in almost every case, both a *personal* responsibility and a *structural* responsibility. All the participants in the harm need to be accountable and accept responsibility individually for what happened; all need to recognize the structural component— the policies, the practices, the social failures, the counter-productive assumptions of hierarchy and punishment—that contributed to the harm, and then, as part of the repair, to *work together* to change what can be changed, deepening relationships along the way.

Repair

No one except the people involved in a harm knows how to repair it. I for one do not know what the participants need until they tell me. But the participants can sit in council together—with whatever help a peacemaker can give—and tell their needs to each other. The topic is simple: *What shall we do to make this right?* Everyone tells complete stories—what happened, how they feel, what they need. The focus is on the future. There is no blaming and no punishing. The goal is for everyone to feel safe enough to be warriors—transparent, vulnerable, courageous, and accountable.

We should never think that peacemaking is simply an excuse for one who has done harm to avoid accountability. In fact, making the person who did the harm accountable is one of the primary goals of the peacemaking process. *How* the person who did the harm will repair it—paying the costs of repair, replacing what was stolen, doing some sort of community service, apologizing, undertaking personally to repair what was broken, proposing concrete steps to prevent the harm from happening again—is something for the circle participants to *work together* to figure out. Here again, we see a conflict reframed. It is no longer the case of an authority deciding on a punishment, but rather a community meeting together to consider how to meet a *mutual unmet need* to repair a harm.

Reintegration

Desmond Tutu, speaking about the South African post-apartheid Truth and Reconciliation Commission, said that its "central concern is the healing of breaches, the redressing of imbalances, the restoration of broken relationships, and a search to rehabilitate both the victim and the perpetrator who should be given the opportunity to be reintegrated into the community by his offense." But perhaps it was Reverend Martin Luther King Jr. who best expressed the idea of reintegration: "The end is reconciliation; the end is redemption; the end is the creation of the beloved community."

The goal of every peacemaking process is redemption for *all* the participants in a harm, for *everyone* to be reintegrated into their community. Remember that both the person harmed and the person who did the harm may be estranged from the community within which the harm took place—the person harmed isolated by shame, humiliation, fear that the harm will be repeated, and fear of being thought wrong, or bad, or crazy for feeling ashamed, vengeful, unforgiving, *unheard;* the person who did the harm isolated by remorse, guilt, ostracism, fear of retaliation, and the unheard need to make things right.

In the reintegration process, the community has its own needs. The community has a need to reintegrate both the person harmed and the person who did the harm; both could be valued members of the community, bringing their own gifts for the good of the whole. The community also needs assurances of its own safety, that the harm will not be repeated, that it is not reintegrating someone who feigns accountability. At the same time, the community may need to take steps to meet the needs of the other participants—the provision of programs of rehabilitation, counseling, or ongoing support; changes in policies or procedures; campaigns of awareness for the community as a whole.

Those are all issues to be discussed in council. In the most extreme case, the council may decide that reintegration is not possible—at least not possible *at that moment.* In some cases, the need of the community to protect itself from an unrepentant and predatory doer of harm may outweigh the community's need for reintegration. But it is for all the participants to decide what commitments it may require for reintegration to have the greatest chance of success.

THE PEACEMAKING COMMUNITY

Let us say a harm has been done—something stolen; something broken; someone injured, hurt, humiliated, betrayed, abused, deprived. Let us look at how two different cultures respond to this harm—a punitive community, like ours, and a peacemaking community, a community of reconciliation and redemption, a *beloved* community. We can outline these responses in the following table:

	Punitive	Peacemaking
Focus	Rules	Harms
Outcome	Punishment	Repairs
Basis	Just Deserts	Needs
Goal	Stigma	Reintegration
Effect	Guilt	Obligation
Model	Justice	Healing

As we have discussed, the focus in a punitive community is on rules and punishments; the goal is to identify and punish the person who broke a rule. In a peacemaking community, however, the focus is on the harm that was done and the way in which all the stakeholders in that harm—the one who did it, the one who suffered it, and the community in which it occurred—can *work together* to repair the harm and restore the bonds of trust broken by the harm.

In the same way, punitive systems often speak transactionally about the rule breaker getting the punishment the rule breaker *deserves*. But for a peacemaking system the repair is based instead on the *needs* of all the stakeholders in the harm, which include, as we have said, the restoration of dignity and self-respect, assurances of future safety, the opportunity to make things right, and the restoration of community. Thus, while a punitive system seeks to stigmatize and reject one who has done harm—often by sequestration in some distant prison—peacemaking seeks to integrate the person who has done the harm back into the community.

There is a distinction, too, to be made between the effects of punitive and peacemaking approaches on one who has done a harm. Punitive systems seek to create a sense of guilt, the sense of oneself as a moral failure, inadequate, lower in the moral hierarchy than the other stakeholders. Peacemaking, on the other hand, is intended to create in one who has done a harm a sense not of guilt but of *obligation*—the obligation to speak honestly from the heart about the harm that was done, to listen devoutly to the community and the one who has been harmed, to accept accountability, and to undertake concrete action to make things right.

The model invoked by a punitive community is what its proponents call *justice,* by which they mean a punitive justice—a backward-looking obsession with fact-finding in order to single out the person who is to be punished. The model invoked by a peacemaker is that of healing a wound in the flesh of the community and in the hearts of both the one harmed and the one who did the harm. In a peacemaking community, the response to a harm is a council circle, the original healing ceremony.

Now stop and think. You are a fallible human person; you have both harmed and been harmed by others; in your fallibility and imperfection, you are under a veil of ignorance as to whether you will harm or be harmed by others in the future. Each of these two communities has its problems and challenges. But in which community would you rather live?

THE MYSTERY OF THE FLASH DRIVE

But again, let me emphasize: we should not view responsibility and repair hierarchically and transactionally as outcomes we demand from the circle process, but rather as possible ways in which communities are strengthened and relationships made deeper. The circle will go where it wants to go, always in the direction of openheartedness, and we should not try to—and ultimately we cannot—force it to go in a direction of our choosing, or give us the sort of outcome that we demand. Here is an example.

In a middle school classroom that regularly held council circles, one of the students—we'll call him John—could not find the flash drive he was certain he had put in his backpack.

He accused others in the class of having stolen it—probably not a bad guess, since hiding the flash drive is just the sort of prank a middle school student might play on a classmate. But all the other students denied having taken it; they said that John had probably lost or misplaced it and was just blaming others for something that was his own fault.

John complained to the teacher, and the story eventually reached the principal, who called the class together and told the person who had taken the flash drive to confess. No one budged; the students all denied having taken the flash drive. The principal threatened to punish the whole class if no one came forward. Again, no one budged, either because no one had in fact taken the flash drive, or because the person who had taken it was quite rationally seeking to evade punishment.

When the principal had departed, the teacher called a council circle to discuss the incident. The students' positions were unchanged. There was an impasse as to the facts—that is, as to who broke the rule, and even what rule had been broken, whether the rule against taking things from other students' backpacks or the rule against blaming others for taking something that you yourself had misplaced.

The first council session, focusing on who did what to whom, eventually ended, by common consent, in frustration.

There were several more circles focusing on this issue, and as the circles continued, the focus almost imperceptibly shifted away from factual disputes into expressions of feelings and needs—how John felt about his loss, how the other students felt about being accused, the need to feel that one's belongings are safe in the classroom, the students' dismay at the disruption of their previously strong community.

After several circles, a remarkable thing happened. *The facts no longer mattered.* It became apparent that all the students, including John, had a *mutual unmet need*—the need to rebuild and maintain the sense of community that was in place before the incident.

So the question of who did what to whom simply faded away. Friendships reconstituted themselves; John simply melted back into the community, which somehow was now stronger than ever.

Sometimes, when I think about this story, I feel a sense of frustration. I want to know: *What the hell happened to the flash drive?* Did someone take it and then, when the prank blew up, discard it out of fear or guilt? Did John find the flash drive on the floor of the closet where he keeps his backpack and stay silent out of embarrassment? Shouldn't somebody confess, apologize, offer to replace the flash drive? And the answer is that I will never know the facts, and *it does not matter.* We will never know the complex interactions that led up to a punch in the school yard; we will never know the causal web that led to three generations of bitter and brutal interethnic warfare in a newly formed nation. All we can do is think like a peacemaker and celebrate the mystery of the process and the beauty of deepening relationships.

12
Revenge

When asked about the needs of one who has been harmed, or of the community in which the harm occurred, people often put forward a claim that a harmed person needs *revenge*. Yet there are limits to this revenge. Most people in North America would not want a thief to be tortured to death. Even the most punitive among us think in terms not just of proportionate but of somehow *appropriate* punishment. The jilted lover wants her betrayer to feel, in turn, the pains of betrayal; a robbery victim who was beaten wants in turn to beat his assailant; the victim of rape anticipates the rapist in turn raped in prison. If we disentangle revenge from the myth of redemptive violence, the purpose of revenge is always something like this: *so he knows what it feels like.* In other words, under the guise of revenge, what we are seeking is a form of accountability.

Why do we think that revenge—hurting and humiliating the person who harmed us—is a good response to harm? Apart from the fact that we have been told over and over again that such violence is redemptive, healing, and praiseworthy,

I think there are several beliefs that contribute to the myth. Violence is an appealing solution to a harm because it appears efficient; we believe that by singling out the blameworthy person for punishment—pain, humiliation, deprivation—we have solved the problem. The solution also has the appearance of being fair; you harm me, so I harm you back, and we have somehow restored balance to the universe. We believe that the harmer is different from us, less human, less understandable, with alien feelings and opaque needs. And we believe that it is possible for us to harm another person without harming ourselves.

These beliefs are all demonstrably false.

You will recall the ending of *The Karate Kid*. The young beleaguered hero, matched in a karate tournament against his tormentor, delivers a knockout kick despite having been injured, unfairly, by his opponent. Here again is the myth of redemptive violence, reinforced in the film by the tormentor, chastened by his defeat, himself presenting the winning trophy to the young hero. Once, when I was teaching a class on nonviolent resistance to a group of middle school students, I asked if they thought this ending was realistic. "Nah," one boy said. "He and his friends will jump him later. With a brick."

The young student showed a keen and uncensored awareness of what have been called *cycles of violence*. The bully will, in fact, smart at his hurt and humiliation and plan retaliatory violence. One needs to have only a superficial knowledge of the long-term intractable interethnic conflicts in today's world to understand that this is true.

Once again, Reverend Martin Luther King Jr. put the idea best: "The way of violence," he wrote, "leads to bitterness in the survivors and brutality in the destroyers." The bitterness and brutality alternate in never-ending cycles. Each side develops its own *narrative of victimization* at the hands of a dehumanized and demonized other. Each side closes its ranks and its heart against the other. Each side says: *They started it.* Each side says: *It's no use to talk to them.* Each side thirsts for revenge, when in reality each side needs *to be heard,* to give voice to its pain, to hold the other *accountable,* to put a stop to the endless violence.

13
Apologizing

When a harm has been done, people often demand an apology from the person who has done the harm. We tend to think that apologies are important because we think about them transactionally: *I will trade you my apology for your forgiveness.* Or even more commonly: *I will trade you my apology for your letting me walk away from accountability.*

On the other hand, when we begin to think transformationally, we can see that apologies are useful only when they help to heal and deepen a broken relationship. Trust can be restored without an explicit apology where there is remorse and a willingness to be accountable. Sometimes a person who has been harmed will express a *need* for an explicit statement of remorse from the person who has caused the harm. This need can be validated and explored. As with revenge, I think the demand for an apology is a transactional substitute for a transformational need—the need to see remorse and accountability. So here, once again, we have a mutual unmet need for *accountability* that can be worked out by speaking honestly and listening devoutly—the need for the person harmed to see and for the person who did the harm to express genuine remorse and a willingness to make things right.

Sometimes people who have harmed another person are not ready to apologize. Instead, they seek to make excuses and to justify the harm they caused: *She was asking for it. He shouldn't have said that. They did it first.* Such excuses and justifications are not necessarily self-centered arbitrary evasions of accountability. They are in fact perfectly rational attempts to avoid punishment. A person who has harmed another in our culture *expects* to be punished, and almost certainly has been punished in the past. It may take awhile in council for the person to understand that what is expected is not punishment but repair, and that part of that repair is to be *accountable*—to express genuine remorse.

An apology needs to be a *healing* apology. A complete apology should do four things—recognize that a harm has been done to the listener; accept responsibility for the speaker's part in the harm; express shame, sorrow, remorse, and, where appropriate, assurances that the harm will not recur; and seek to repair the harm. Here is a simple example:

◇ I broke the dish that you lent to me.
◇ I should have been more careful.
◇ I am really sorry. I feel terrible.
◇ I will replace it before we meet again.

There are therefore four ways in which an apology can go wrong, and be worse than no apology at all.

First, a bad apology may fail to recognize that a harm was actually done, or fail to recognize that it was done to the person being apologized to. The apology may state the harm hypothetically: *If I offended you . . .* or vaguely: *Whatever I did to offend you . . .* or may state the harm without recognizing that it was done to the person being apologized to: *If anyone was offended. . . .* The apology may be made to someone other than the person harmed, and for something other than the harm actually done: *I apologize to my family for embarrassing them.*

Second, a bad apology may evade responsibility. An apology in the passive voice, for example, is invariably intended to obscure the speaker's agency: *I regret that mistakes were made.* A bad apology may ignore the harm that was actually done, and instead apologize for something else: *I am sorry to have made an error in judgment.* A bad apology may even blame the listener: *I am sorry you are so upset.*

Third, the apology may fail to express remorse, or may offer no assurance that the harm will not be repeated. We are used to hearing—and accepting—a perfunctory *I'm sorry* with no genuine sorrow behind it.

Fourth, the apology may fail to offer to repair the harm, which includes a proposal for ensuring that the harm does not recur. Usually this part of a complete apology is just left out. Because the apology is seen as part of a transaction, a person who has harmed another may think that the apology itself is sufficient repair. In some cases, this may be correct, but that is up to the listener to decide, not the one apologizing.

Thus, an adequate apology—a *complete* apology—might look like this: *I'm sorry I was late. I know how much that bothers you. From now on I'll leave home fifteen minutes earlier, and I'll call you if I'm delayed.* Or again: *I'm sorry I shouted at you. I had a really bad day, but I still should not have taken it out on you. From now on, if I'm feeling tense when I get home, I will take a walk around the block before I come in the door.*

If the one apologizing cannot think of an adequate repair, then the apology can simply ask: *What can I do to make this right?* These words recognize the mutual unmet need that both parties have to see that their relationship is repaired, and that trust and harmony have been restored.

14
Forgiving

We have very complex attitudes toward forgiveness in our culture. Forgiveness is often seen as part of a transaction: *I will trade you my forgiveness for your apology.* Forgiveness in our culture is often hierarchical: the person who forgives becomes morally superior to the one forgiven. Indeed, we are sometimes told we have an *obligation* to forgive, and if we can't forgive a rape, a killing, a genocide, then we are ourselves moral failures. At the same time, forgiveness is often dismissed as weak and foolish, encouraging repetition of the harm that has been forgiven, and inconsistent with the foundational myth of redemptive violence.

Still, forgiveness can be miraculous. Here is a true story, which was told to us at a seminar on restorative dialogue in cases of severe political and criminal violence, given by Mark Umbreit of the University of Minnesota's Center for Restorative Justice and Peacemaking. Jane's sister had been raped and murdered by David, who was subsequently convicted of the crime and sentenced to life in prison. For years

Jane carried such furious and impotent rage at the man who had killed her sister that it affected her health and her marriage. Fifteen years after the man had been convicted, she developed what she saw as a strange need to talk with him, and she was amazed to find that programs were in place to help facilitate such dialogues.

Her initial goal was twofold. She wanted to let the man know the harm he had done, the kind of life he had snuffed out, the impact he had had on the friends and family of the victim—in other words, to be accountable, to *know how it felt.* And she wanted factual information—why he had chosen her sister to rape and kill, whether it had somehow been her fault, what her last words had been.

Such meetings take a tremendous amount of preparation. It took a year of circles with Jane and David separately before they were ready to meet in council with each other. David knew that his participation in the meeting with Jane would have no effect on any possible parole or on the conditions of his incarceration. Jane was ready to meet the man her fear and anger had painted as a faceless monster. David was ready to be accountable for the harm he had done. A prison conference room was set aside for the meeting. A guard would be stationed outside, and a support person for Jane would be present throughout the meeting.

Jane brought with her a picture of her sister, which she put on the table in front of David. The meeting was going as planned. Jane was telling her story—her loss, her grief, her rage, her need for understanding. And David was telling his story as well—his confusion, his remorse, his hopelessness, the inner demons that drove him to harm others, his life in prison.

But suddenly, Jane says, the room was filled with angels. She heard a voice say to her, clearly and distinctly: *If you're going to do it, do it now.* So she turned to David, and to the amazement of both of them, she said: *I forgive you.* Jane says it was like a physical weight leaving her body, as both she and David cried out in their mutual grief.

I cannot tell you how often that metaphor recurs in stories of forgiveness. People say it is like a weight being lifted, a burden laid down, a sense of lightness and freedom, like suddenly flying.

It can take a long time before one is ready to make this leap. At the same seminar, another woman spoke about the murder of her son in a gang-related shooting at a park. At the sentencing phase of the trial of her son's killer, she said, in her victim impact statement, that she had forgiven the young man, since she was a Christian woman. And she says: *Of course that was not true.* It was not until many years later, when they both were ready and prepared for their face-to-face meeting, that she truly forgave him and laid down her burden of rage.

As with apologies, forgiveness is not always necessary, in the sense that, in some cases, trust and harmony can be restored without it. But forgiveness may be necessary, in two ways. First, forgiving—welcoming the person who did the harm back into a healed relationship—may be an unmet need of the person harmed. And second, *receiving* forgiveness—knowing that remorse and apology have been accepted as genuine—may be an unmet need of the person who did the harm.

I believe that forgiveness is a deep and primal human response to genuine remorse. That is one reason that true apologies can be so important and so powerful: they prepare the ground for forgiveness. But as with speaking and listening, apologizing and forgiving interact in complex and synergistic ways. Just as a genuine apology can open the heart to forgiveness, genuine forgiveness can open the heart to remorse. Most important, in the vast majority of cases, conflicts and harms occur in the context of ongoing relationships that are not easy to punctuate. In such cases, apologies and forgiveness can come from both sides and be mutually reinforcing. All the parties to a conflict—even a long and violent one—can lay down their burdens together.

Forgiveness does not condone or approve or forget the harmful acts. Forgiveness does not mean allowing yourself to be abused; forgiving does not give permission for the behavior to be repeated. Forgiveness does not mean that what was done was acceptable; indeed, forgiveness is needed precisely for actions that were not acceptable. Forgiveness is the ultimate expression of St. Francis's transformed and undefended heart. To disarm oneself in the face of violence is an act of profoundest courage.

Forgiveness is risky. Where violence has occurred—murder, rape, a terrorist attack—it can take decades before someone who has been harmed is ready to take that risk. And even then it can take years of active preparation before one who has been harmed by violence is ready to embrace a need to forgive. In part this is due to our cultural teachings that contradict the deeply human impulse to forgive. In part it is because the person needs a sacred space—a *healing circle*—within which one who has been harmed by violence can think through and articulate this impulse.

15
Healing Circles

Circles that bring together someone who has done a harm and the person who has been harmed are often called something like *victim-offender conferences,* a term that unnecessarily reinforces the Manichean assumptions of a punitive and hierarchical culture. Harms range from those done by intimate partners to those done by acquaintances, community members, or utter strangers committing acts of rape or terrorism on people they do not know at all, and it would be preferable to use a term that can encompass all these cases. I propose the term *healing circle* or *healing council,* but what the council will be called is, of course, up to the participants.

Healing circles can consist of just a few participants—the one who did the harm, the person harmed, a community member, a peacemaker—up to circles that consist of those participants as well as family, friends, and community representatives, which may include social workers, law enforcement, and prosecutors. All are committed to enter the sacred space and time of council with the intention to bring healing and reconciliation rather than judgment and punishment.

In almost all cases, when there has been proper preparation and commitment to the process, it is better for the person who did the harm and the person harmed to meet face-to-face. People who have been harmed, working in council with a peacemaker, have to think through exactly what it is they want to gain from the circle. Sometimes this is just information. The person harmed may ask: *Why did you choose me? Was it somehow my fault? What was it that made you do this?* Sometimes there is a need to tell the person who did the harm the extent of the harm done, the pain, the injury, the inconvenience, the fear, the isolation, the continuing stress. Sometimes there is a need to see remorse or receive an apology. The peacemaker needs to make sure these needs are realistic and, based on similar work with the person who did the harm, possible to achieve.

People who have harmed another also work with the peacemaker to create realistic expectations. Those incarcerated must be willing to go through the process for its own sake, not in order to gain a reduction in sentence or improvement in the conditions of incarceration. They have to be very clear about what they want—a chance to explain, a way to express remorse, a desire for forgiveness, an opportunity, in whatever small way, to make things right.

Sometimes these preliminary sessions reveal that the participants are just not yet ready to sit together in council. The person harmed may express an interest in meeting with the person who did the harm but may express unrealistic expectations for the outcome of the circle; the person who did the harm may refuse to be accountable, or may be feigning interest in order to be able to use the fact of meeting before the parole board. What this means is that the participants are not ready for a healing circle *at that moment*. If either one is not really ready, then the circle cannot take place. It is impossible to say that such lack of readiness will remain unchanged forever.

There are cases where such face-to-face meetings are unlikely to work, especially where there has been a significant power differential between the person who did the harm and the person harmed, and even more where that power differential is the result of violence—cases such as a torturer and the person tortured, a rapist and the person raped.

Even here, though, healing circles are possible. One prison has set up a system for persons who have been raped to meet in circle with rapists—not the person who raped them, but rather who have raped others. These rapists and persons raped, with proper preparation, can open their hearts to each other in council, the people raped telling the complete stories of their experience and its aftermath, the rapists speaking honestly from their hearts about their demons and remorse.

It is natural for those of us raised in a hierarchical, punitive, and transactional culture to be skeptical about such healing circles. Yet there are cultures where such peacemaking is accepted as natural. Diane LaResche is a university lecturer in conflict resolution and a tribal peacemaking consultant. In a special issue of *The Mediation Quarterly* devoted to peacemaking among indigenous peoples, she writes that indigenous peacemaking is not so much concerned with retributive or distributive justice as it is with *sacred justice*. "Sacred justice is found," she says, "when the importance of restoring understanding and balance to relationships has been acknowledged." A peacemaking process is thus a "guiding process," a *relationship-healing* journey to assist people in returning to harmony.

In the same issue, Philmer Bluehouse, a Navajo and coordinator of the Navajo Peacemaker Court, and James Zion, a solicitor to the Courts of the Navajo Nation, write: "The Peacemaker wonders, 'Is it *hashhkeeji* (moving toward disharmony) or is it *hozhooji* (moving towards harmony)?'" Zion provides a summary of the Navajo peacemaking court: "The parties talk out their problem and how they feel about it to gain empathy and, at the end, consensus on how to realign their relationships in a meaningful way."

The Diné word *hozho* connotes a complex of meanings— healing, harmony, balance, beauty, right relationship. When the rains come in season and the four sacred crops grow, there is both harmony and beauty in the world. When the people maintain right relationships with each other, with the plants and animals, and with the sacred world, there is both harmony and beauty in the world. You have probably read the Navajo prayer:

With beauty before me, may I walk.
With beauty behind me, may I walk.
With beauty above me, may I walk.
With beauty below me, may I walk.
With beauty all around me, may I walk.

When a Navajo has been in combat, or has killed a fellow human, it is said that his *hozho*, his harmony, his beauty has been lost, and it must be restored through a sing called the Beautyway, the Way of *Hozho*. It is striking that, while we tend to call our legal forums something like Courts of Justice, the traditional Navajo peacemaking court is called *hozhooji naat'aanii* or *Leading Toward Harmony*. As James Zion describes the difference, "Western law is based on punishment, and Indian law is based on healing."

Rupert Ross—for many years a Crown Attorney among the native peoples of Canada and an explorer into indigenous peacemaker justice—reports that such councils among First Nations in Canada have offered resolution for even the most intractable of harms—alcoholism, addiction, family abuse, even child sexual abuse, all born of poverty, despair, and loss of culture.

PART III

❋

*Walking
the Peace Path*

16
Why Council Works

If you have experience with council, then you know that it works. Participants do in fact open their hearts, listen devoutly, and speak honestly. Circles become communities. Conflicts and tensions appear and are absorbed into deeper relationships. How in the world does this happen?

I think the answer to that question lies in the deepest part of human nature. Council works because human persons have three inherent characteristics:

◇ Humans have a need to be in right relationship with each other.
◇ Humans are autonomous self-healing problem solvers.
◇ Humans are the best experts on their own needs and situations.

If these statements were not true, then council would not work. If these statements *are* true, then the consequences are revolutionary.

Think about it for a moment. If these statements are true,

then we must reconsider all the assumptions we have learned in a hierarchical, punitive, and transactional culture. In situations of indecision, doubt, conflict, and violence, people do not need to be told what to do. People are able to resolve their doubts and conflicts and enmities for *themselves,* as long as they are able to sit together in sacred space and time. It is the job of the peacemaker simply to create and hold a space in which the antagonists can listen devoutly and speak honestly to each other.

Much of our culture—our hierarchies, our punishments, our transactions—is based on the denial of one or more of these three statements. And indeed, when we step outside the sacred space and time of council the statements certainly appear to be false. People destroy their relationships of trust and confidence over seemingly minor matters; people act against their own best interests; people stay mired in their unresolved problems and conflicts for years.

Outside the sacred space and time of council, people do behave in these self-defeating ways. But the conclusion that is drawn from this observation—that people are *not,* in fact, autonomous self-healing problem solvers—is incorrect. Unproductive or apparently harmful behavior can often be seen as problem-solving behavior that happens to be unsuccessful; and unsuccessful problem solving in turn is most often the result of insufficient information, outside pressure, a need to reduce the stress of a problem as quickly as possible, or simply the lack of a safe space within which to work out better solutions.

If people require sacred space and sacred time to reach their inherent personhood, then the problem is not the limitation of humans but rather the lack of sacred space and time. If our culture—hierarchical, punitive, and transactional—can create conditions outside of council that keep people from autonomy, healing, and problem solving, then the answer is not to scorn their inherent strengths, but rather *to expand the boundaries of the circle.*

How do we do that? Let's begin with the simplest type of council—a two-person circle. In fact, one of the most productive uses of council is simply when two people meet together, both holding the intentions of council, in order to share, discuss, decide, deal with a conflict, or deepen their relationship. There is no describing the depth that can be won by two people just taking turns listening devoutly and speaking from their hearts.

The two-person circle is a key to nurturing and sustaining a long-term relationship between two people. The more often two people meet together in council, the more honest speaking and devout listening becomes an inherent part of their relationship. At some point, just meeting becomes a ceremony, and just being together becomes a circle; they live together in their own sacred space and sacred time.

17
The Invisible Talking Stick

THE NATURE OF THE INVISIBLE TALKING STICK

In the openhearted, intimate two-person council, the partici-pants may on occasion hand each other a real, physical talking stick, but they need not. What they hand each other is an *invisible talking stick*.

We have been talking about passing the talking stick, and we have been assuming that it is a real, solid, visible stick. But it is important to understand that this stick can be invisible, and that it is possible to hand this invisible talking stick to someone without that person even knowing. It is the posses-sion of the invisible talking stick that in many ways defines peacemaking as a spiritual path.

When we talk to another person, and we hand that per-son our invisible talking stick, we are committing to the four intentions of council. As long as that person holds that stick, our intention is to listen devoutly with our heart. As long as that person holds the stick, we listen devoutly to silence, and we listen devoutly to speaking that may—to us, in our ignorance—seem rambling or inconsequential. When that person stops speaking, we wait a moment to make sure that the speaking is finished, and we say a silent *aho!* in our heart, and we give a visible affirmation—perhaps a nod or a whispered *good*—indicating that we recognize the courage it took to hold our invisible stick. Then we take back the invisible talking stick and speak to that person honestly from our heart, spontaneously and with lean expression. And then we hand back the invisible stick.

We can also use the invisible talking stick to tell our complete stories to another. A parent might hold her invisible talking stick to her heart and tell a complete story to an adolescent child:

> *I noticed you were late coming home to dinner from school today. I know that you sometimes have to work at the library, and I know that you really like to hang out with your friends. When that happens, I don't know what to do about dinner. And I worry about you. I need to know that you are safe, and I need to know when you will be home. I need to talk with you about ways we can do that.*

And then the parent can hand the adolescent the invisible talking stick, and listen devoutly to what the teenager has to say.

Having told a complete story, having put out there

both feelings and needs, it is the devout listening that now makes the difference. It may be that the teenager has never felt listened to before; it may be that much of the teenager's difficult behavior has been an unarticulated attempt to be heard. When the parent hands over the invisible talking stick and sits patiently with the intentions of the council circle, there is a shift away from the dynamic of previous interactions. Maybe there will be a solution worked out—perhaps an agreement that the teenager will text the mother her plans right after school every day. But as we should know by now, *the solution is the least important part of the process.*

What is important here is the honest speaking and devout listening. What is important is for the adolescent to hear the mother's feelings and needs, to understand that the mother is not arbitrarily exercising her power to constrict the teenager's life but has a genuine and loving concern for the teenager's safety. And what is important is for the mother to listen devoutly with her heart to her teenager's need for autonomy, with respect for her judgment— her need *to be heard.*

The effect of using an invisible talking stick is miraculous. Family members whose interactions have for years consisted of arguing, yelling, and slamming doors suddenly find themselves talking about their feelings and needs. Strangers open their hearts and tell us their amazing stories. Life becomes more interesting. Fear begins to vanish. The invisible talking stick slowly and magically transforms its bearer into a peacemaker.

GETTING YOUR
INVISIBLE TALKING STICK

I want to take you on a short journey. We are going to meet your own individual Inner Peacemaker, who will give you the gift of your invisible talking stick.

The Inner Peacemaker is the most deeply human part of ourselves, the one within us who shows us how to live in right relationship with all other beings. The Inner Peacemaker looks different to different people; in fact, the Inner Peacemaker may appear in different ways to the same person at different times. As we go on our visit, we should not try to guess ahead of time what the Inner Peacemaker will look like—a human, an animal, a form of smoke. We should give ourselves permission to be surprised.

Close your eyes. Get comfortable. As you relax more and more deeply, you suddenly find yourself on a forest trail. Look around you. Look at the trees, the sunshine refracted through the green leaves, the splash of sunlight on the forest floor. Smell the forest smell, listen to the rustling of the leaves and the calling of distant birds, touch the rough bark of a tree trunk, feel the solid ground beneath your feet and the touch of wind on your skin. Use all your senses. Walk down the path in the forest, enjoying all these sensations and a feeling of peace.

Soon you come to a small stream running across the path. You go down the bank, splash across the stream, and come up the other side onto the path again. You realize that the stream marks the boundary between an ordinary forest and a *magical* forest, and you know that by crossing the stream you are now in the forest of myths and dreams.

As you continue to walk on the path, the sun begins to set. The quality of the light changes, the birds slowly stop singing, and the air takes on a pleasant chill. It is getting darker and darker, and it is becoming more difficult to follow the path. As darkness falls, you see ahead a bright spot of light, and you realize that the path is taking you toward a campfire in a forest clearing.

You come to the edge of the clearing, and you ask for permission to enter. As you enter into the circle of firelight you see your Inner Peacemaker seated quietly on a log. Now you can see what your Inner Peacemaker looks like, at least during this meeting. What does it mean to you that the Inner Peacemaker is appearing to you now in this form? You sit down on the log and ask a question, spontaneous and unprepared, or sit silently, listening devoutly with your heart. Let time pass. Speak to your Inner Peacemaker honestly from your heart, and listen devoutly to the response.

After a while, you realize that you have been sitting with your Inner Peacemaker through the whole night. The sky is becoming lighter; birds have started to sing. You know it is time to leave. Before you go, say to your Inner Peacemaker: *Please give me a gift for my people.* Hold out your hand.

Your Inner Peacemaker places in your hand a talking stick that is invisible to everyone but you. Feel it in your hand; feel its weight, its heft. Look at it, see whether it is decorated or plain, touch its surface, look at its colors. Over time, this talking stick will become clearer and clearer to all your senses. For now, you put it in your pocket, thank your Inner Peacemaker, and ask if you may come back again. The

Inner Peacemaker says: *You can always return, any time you wish. Just cross the stream into the magic forest, and you will find me waiting for you.*

You walk away from the clearing, down the path. The sun is rising, the birds are singing, the leaves are rustling in the morning breeze. You smell the fragrance of the awakening forest. You cross the little stream back into the ordinary forest, and as you walk down the forest path you slowly awaken where you are sitting, with your invisible talking stick in your pocket.

Now that you have it, what do you do with it?

WALK WITH A TALKING STICK

A peacemaker *walks through life with a talking stick.* Peacemakers hand their invisible sticks to everyone they meet—friends, relatives, taxi drivers, store clerks, trees, rocks, thunder. When you walk with a talking stick, everything becomes an encounter, a genuine meeting, and every encounter becomes an opportunity to listen devoutly and speak honestly from your heart.

Hand your talking stick to people. You can hand your talking stick to your family, friends, and coworkers. But if you want an adventure, hand your talking stick to a stranger. Your taxi driver, your fellow passenger on the bus, the man standing in front of you at the checkout line, the woman on a park bench feeding the pigeons, the man wearing the pinstripe suit waiting for the commuter train—I guarantee you that they all have the most marvelous stories to tell you, and that they will, perhaps to your surprise, be willing to listen devoutly to the stories you tell in return. Ask a simple question, hand over your talking stick, and see what happens.

And here is a remarkable thing. As you hand your invisible talking stick to more and more people, it will begin to be automatic. You will hand your talking stick to *everyone*. You will invite miracles into your life and walk every day in the beauty of human joy and sorrow.

Hand your talking stick to the natural world. I am not being metaphorical here. Go out into the woods and find a huge old moss-covered rock, or a wise old grandfather tree. Ask the rock or tree for permission to speak with it; ask if it will be your teacher. Then hold the talking stick in your hand and tell your story. Make it a *complete* story—how you feel, what you need, what you regret, what you fear. Then hand the stick to the rock or tree and *listen,* devoutly, with your heart, to the story the rock or tree will tell you. It may take a while, but you will hear it.

Hand your talking stick to the spirits. The whole world wants to speak to us, but we do not listen devoutly with our hearts. Whether we know it or not, we humans live in community with persons who are not human beings. These other-than-human persons may include animals, plants, trees, rocks, clouds, thunder, and stars. We sit with all of them, whether we know it or not, in a great talking circle. The goal is for us to pass our talking stick back and forth, speak to these others honestly from our hearts, and listen devoutly with our hearts to what they seek to teach us. To sit in this great talking circle with humility and gratitude is our common and most profound human heritage.

The phrase *other-than-human persons* was coined by anthropologist Irving Hallowell to describe the world of the Ojibwe, in which humans, animals, fish, birds, and plants— and some rocks, trees, and storms—are all relational, intentional, conscious, and communicative beings. Ethnographer Thomas Blackburn reached similar conclusions for the Chumash Indians, whose cosmos, he said, is composed of an "interacting community of sentient creatures." Cultural ecologist David Abram speaks of "the intuition that every form one perceives . . . is an experiencing form, an entity with its own predilections and sensations."

These other-than-human persons are recognized in a variety of ways—whether they can be talked with, whether gifts can be exchanged with them, and whether they can be engaged in a cultural system of respect and reciprocity. Find an ancient rock, give it a gift of tobacco, ask if it will be your teacher, hand it your invisible talking stick, and listen devoutly to the gift it gives you in return—its story, its song, a ceremony, a dream.

This is to live with what anthropologist Nurit Bird-David has called a "relational epistemology." Anthropologist Enrique Salmón, himself a Tarahumara, calls this a *kincentric ecology*—"an awareness that life in any environment is viable only when humans view the life surrounding them as kin."

In the same way, we can hand our talking stick to the one spirit that is everywhere, under whatever name—Spirit, or the Sacred, or the Source, or Creator, or *Gitche Manitou*, Great Spirit, or *Wakan Tanka*, That-Which-Is-Mysterious-and-

Alive. When we hand our talking stick to the spirits, or to the Sacred, we are in council. We do not ask to be fixed, or saved, or healed, or transformed; we pour out our open hearts—our fears, regrets, needs, worries, hopes; and then we hand over our talking stick and listen devoutly with our hearts to what the spirits say in return.

Hand your talking stick to your dreams and visions. The things we encounter in our dreams are just like human and other-than-human persons, and we can hand them our talking stick, listen devoutly to what they say, and tell them our innermost stories in return. This should not surprise us. We often think this way about our dreams. We ask: *What is this dream saying to me?* We dream we are in a locker room. We assume that, because it is in a dream, the locker room has meaning that it is speaking to us. We ask: *What does it mean to be in a locker room?* And we answer: *A locker room is a place where you change,* or, *A locker room is a place where you are naked.*

This is how we can use our talking stick in our dreams. I dream I am inside a house, trying to escape some formless terror. I reach the door, pull it open, and there before me is another huge menacing shape, blocking my escape. I wake up full of fear, my heart pounding. So I go back into the dream, or I call up before me the menacing shape in the doorway. I hand it my talking stick—perhaps my *dream* talking stick, full of magic—and I ask: *Who are you? What do you want from me? Will you tell me what you mean? Will you be my teacher?*

Suppose you dream that you are walking on a path,

trip over a rock, and look up to see a child holding a flower and smiling at you. The dream is salient and powerful; it seems to you to be what some call a Big Dream, mythic and meaningful.

There are many ways you might reflect upon what this dream means and what its significance might be for you. You might go back into the dream to meet the child or sit quietly and invite the child to come to you in a vision, and ask, *Who are you? Why are you smiling? Will you be my teacher?* Or you can ask the rock, *Who are you? Why did you trip me? What lesson are you teaching me?* Then hand the child, the rock, the flower your talking stick, and listen devoutly with your heart to what is said.

And just as we can hand our talking stick to a threatening figure in our dreams, we can also hand it to our pain, our fear, our sorrow, our regret. Ask yourself: *What do I fear?* Call it before you; see what it looks like; hand it your talking stick and say, *Who are you? What do you want from me? Will you be my teacher?* Speak honestly from your heart to your fear or regret or sorrow, and then listen devoutly with your heart to what it tells you.

Hand your talking stick to the concrete events of your life.
Let us go even further with our listening and listen to the *concrete events in our lives.* Those events teach us about ourselves and how to choose the right path on our journeys. It is in listening devoutly to these events that we hear the call of how we should live.

Think again about the dream of the child, the rock, and the flower. Now suppose that exactly the same events occur while you are awake. One day you walk along, trip over a rock, and see the smiling child. Why is that experience any less meaningful—any less salient and mythic—than the same events in a dream? Why do we show our waking experiences the disrespect of dismissing them, when we should respect them as much as we do our dreams? Rather, we should give our waking experiences the same respect we give our dream experiences—hand them our talking stick and take them as our teachers: rich, deep, and full of meaning.

Think of what happened to you today, or yesterday. Put it in the form of a story. If this were the story of a dream, then what is it saying to you? What is the meaning of what happened to you today or yesterday? Is the whole world speaking to you—the rock you tripped over, the child who smiled at you, the rain and moon? Are you listening? This is how we make the world meaningful, and full of mystery.

Hand your talking stick to your whole life. We can compare this process to a vision quest. During a vision quest we leave our ordinary life and comforts behind; we stay in solitude in the wilderness for four days and four nights without a tent or food or fire. In this way we express not only our willingness to undergo hardship for the sake of the spirits but also our separation from our normal social relationships. The voluntary privations are part of our newly liminal condition, in which we encounter the dangerous unknown in order to bring back a gift—a song, a ceremony, our own unguessed talent—not for ourselves but for our people.

When I have undertaken vision quests in the desert, and when I have helped others to do their own vision quests, we often did a small ritual. On our way to the place each of us had chosen for our fast, we would pause and draw a line ahead of us on the path. When we stepped over that line, we knew that we had crossed over into the land of myth and fairy tale, where we would meet ogres and helpers, where every experience—ravens circling in the sky, a cloud drifting across the silver desert moon—became magical and miraculous, spoke to us if we listened devoutly with our heart.

All our encounters make demands on us, and the demands are all the same. We can evade these demands, pretend they do not exist, but the obligations are real. We must be transparent, and vulnerable, and courageous, and accountable. When we encounter others, we must pass them our talking stick, we must speak honestly and listen devoutly for what they are saying to us, in signs and whispers and silent motions of the heart, as if they were the mysterious songs of dreams and visions.

Any encounter is risky and meaningful. We must be willing to undertake the dangerous opening of our hearts, to tell our stories with openhearted honesty, and to listen devoutly with our hearts to what the others tell us in return, often through the merest signs, the inchoate movements of our own hearts, the silent singing of the earth.

In a council circle we do not ask or demand that the others in the circle help us or heal us or change us. We speak honestly from our hearts; we express our fears and hopes and regrets, and we listen to the songs and stories of the others, opening up our hearts, becoming, in a mysterious and sacred process, better people. Sitting in circle with others is itself the healing.

In any encounter, sitting in circle with others, we seek meaning and depth in our encounters. We always encounter the spirits; the world has the depth and meaning of our dreams, and we are on a vision quest always, even in our most routine activities.

The whole world sits with us in a great talking circle. We pass the talking stick back and forth as we tell each other our stories, as we sing each other our songs, as we give our gifts to each other. In a true meeting with another person—a human, a spirit, a rock—we do not seek any end other than genuineness in our meeting.

18
Walking the Peace Path

Nobody says you have to act as a peacemaker. Being a peacemaker is not easy. It requires a change in basic cultural assumptions. It means giving up hierarchy, power, ego, anger, and the comforting myth of redemptive violence. It means a continual commitment and a willingness to accept our inevitable failures. It means being disarmed in an armed world.

To be a peacemaker means being transparent, vulnerable, courageous, and accountable. I think of these as being *warrior virtues,* and they are not prized in our punitive culture. Warriors for peace put themselves out there, in the midst of conflict and mess, with the courage to be openhearted and disarmed.

We cannot just be tourists in sacred space and sacred time. Ultimately, the sacred makes demands on us, and involves us in change, challenge, and sacrifice. We are confronted with questions—how to live in the presence of mystery, how to wrestle with the sacred, how to live out our humanity in the face of conflict, suffering, and failure.

Here are six ways that may help you walk the peace path:

◇ Treat everyone with radical equality
◇ Carry peace with you everywhere
◇ Embrace process
◇ Love ceremony
◇ Be a clown for peace
◇ Walk in beauty every day

TREAT EVERYONE WITH RADICAL EQUALITY

Instead of hierarchy, a peacemaker deploys a *radical egalitarianism* that recognizes and values the unique gifts of every person. A peacemaker truly believes that all people are, inherently, autonomous self-healing problem solvers, and treats them that way.

One of the characteristics of our hierarchical and punitive culture is that we make distinctions between the good and the bad, the victim and the offender, the oppressed and the oppressor; and then we demonize, punish, harm, and stigmatize the ones we have labeled as bad. Especially when a person has caused harm and suffering, we dehumanize the person, cast him out, see him as a creature of alien feelings and opaque needs.

The United States Army Special Forces—the Green Berets—have a motto: *De oppresso liber:* to free the oppressed. This is a wonderful sentiment; freeing the oppressed is noble work. But a peacemaker takes one further step, and seeks *to liberate the oppressor as well.* Reverend Martin Luther King

Jr. acknowledged that Southern white racists were themselves caught up in and oppressed by the systematic oppression of Southern blacks. As Ricky Sherover-Marcuse has pointed out, the role of oppressor, despite its positive reinforcements and material benefits, is a painful experience, one that brings its own constriction, powerlessness, and despair. Under an oppressive regime, oppressed and oppressor have a mutual unmet need for freedom.

Rupert Ross speaks of an Ojibwa teaching that all children are born with four gifts. They might be good runners or good hockey players. They might be good listeners who can take burdens from other people. They might be able to make children feel comfortable and safe. Everyone is to be respected for their gifts, for all gifts are sacred. All people bring something special to the group, and at the same time they all depend on others for the strengths, skills, and knowledge that they lack. A peacemaker, in George Fox's words, sees "that of God in everyman," and knows that every individual brings special talents and insights into the council circle and into the lives of others.

A peacemaker knows that these five things are true of everyone:

We all suffer. We all live, not on the mountain peak of spirit, but in the valley of the soul, amid anger, love, envy, resentment, grief, sorrow, loss, and mess. Everyone gets sick, grows old, and dies. Everyone has suffered the loss of love; everyone has been deprived of things they need; everyone has failed. Everyone has been harmed, and everyone has harmed another. In this we are all the same. Recognizing this is part of devout listening to another person's complete story—the person's needs, fears, regrets, shame, sorrows.

We are all sacred. At the same time, there is that which is sacred in everyone—what Quaker George Fox called "that of God in everyman," what Buddhists call our innate Buddha nature. This too is part of a person's complete story—the deeply felt human need to be in right relationship, to make amends, to forgive.

We are all bound together. Buddhist monk and peace activist Thich Nhat Hanh translates the ancient Buddhist concept of *pratītyasamutpāda,* dependent origination, with the wonderful expression *interbeing.* Everything that exists is interwoven with everything else in a great web of causes and conditions. "When we realize our nature of interbeing," he says, "we will stop blaming and killing, because we know that we inter-are." Peacemaker John Paul Lederach articulates the same idea. "The moral imagination," he writes, "requires us to imagine ourselves in a web of relationships that includes our enemies . . . to sustain a paradoxical curiosity that embraces complexity without reliance on dualistic polarity."

We are all fallible. We all make mistakes; we all harm others; we all often fail to live up to our own best selves. We make mistakes because we lack information, we lack time, we lack people who will listen to us with their hearts and give us a space within which we can discern our true nature. A peacemaker recognizes that the same thing is true of those who harm us or have harmed others.

We are all capable of redemption. Everyone is capable of unlearning hierarchy, giving up punishment, seeking transformative rather than transactional human relationships. We are all able to create our own islands of sacred space and time.

CARRY PEACE
WITH YOU EVERYWHERE

I believe that the most powerful way of teaching is by *modeling*—that is, by demonstrating what we want the other person to learn. If we want people to learn peacemaking, then we must, as Daniel Bowling and David Hoffman put it, *bring peace into the room.*

People who are just beginning to use their invisible talking stick often complain that the other person, when handed the invisible stick, just keeps talking and doesn't listen. I have two responses to this. First, I say: Good. The other person is talking. That's what you wanted to happen. The person probably has a lot to say, because no one has ever really listened before. Second, I say: All the time the other person is talking, you are teaching the other person how to listen. You do it by listening, and the other person learns from you how to do it.

Listening is contagious. Listening devoutly and speaking honestly are authentically human ways to be, and people respond to them. Speaking honestly from the heart compels listening; listening devoutly with the heart compels honest speaking.

Mohandas Gandhi famously said, "We must be the change we want to see in the world." George Fox, the founder of the Quakers in the seventeenth century, put the same thought this way:

> Be patterns, be examples in all countries, places, islands, nations, wherever you come; that your carriage and life may preach among all sorts of people, and to them. Then you will come to walk cheerfully over the world, answering that of God in everyone.

EMBRACE PROCESS

Throughout this book, we have distinguished *process* from *product.* Because our culture views human relationships transactionally, we have been taught to see products as being very important. We think in terms of resolutions, solutions, agreements, contracts, compromises, apologies, punishments. That in turn leads us to be frustrated and impatient when such products are not forthcoming. And that frustration is compounded by our belief that conflict is bad and must be resolved as quickly as possible.

Once we start to think about human relationships transformationally, however, we begin to see that relationships are *processes,* not products. Embracing process makes us patient. I often have to remind myself: *People are all exactly where they are supposed to be.* I do not know where you are on your journey. But if I am going to meet you, I have to meet you where you are, not where I think you should be.

I have seen council circles get filled with frustration and disappointment because something was supposed to happen—a resolution, an agreement, a solution. People in the circle were so focused on *getting somewhere* that they forgot to listen for spirit, for the deepening of their relationship, for the tiny birds and insects teaching them on their vision quest. But it is *getting somewhere* just to sit quietly in sacred time together. It is *getting somewhere* just to hear someone hold the stick and say: *I am sad today.*

Christian pacifist Abraham Johannes Muste said, "There is no way to peace. Peace is the way." Buddhist monk and peace activist Thich Nhat Hanh said, "Peace is every step." What these wise elders are telling us is that we must *embrace process.* Because we live in a transactional culture, we are constantly seeking to secure outcomes. When people are in apparent conflict, we seek negotiation, compromise, something for something. We seek a solution, rather than a deepening relationship.

But sometimes in a conflict, or where a harm has been done, a person is not ready to be accountable, not ready to work, not ready to commit. Council can only open those doors that are ready to open; it cannot kick them down. This too is part of a process. A person may sit in circle many times, silent and afraid, and then, suddenly, the dam may break and deeply held truths come pouring out. We trust the process to give all the participants exactly what they need *at that moment,* to meet them where they are.

Embracing process also means remaining open to the unknown, mysterious, and confusing, being aware of our ignorance, avoiding easy answers. It means learning to be present to suffering, recognizing our avoidance and denial of suffering in ourselves and others.

Being a peacemaker is also a process, one that never

ends. We recognize that we often fail to live up to our own best selves. We understand that we are often in the grip of a punitive and violent mythology. We know that the anger messenger will often knock at our door. We do not become peacemakers; rather, we set out to walk on the peacemaking path. We are always *on the way,* always in process.

Finally, making peace in the world is also a process. I am skeptical of large projects. An industrial chemist will tell you that processes that work just fine on a small scale often mysteriously do not work when scaled up to industrial levels. I am skeptical of government and of large nonprofit agencies. I believe that we should build tiny islands of peace in our punitive and hierarchical ocean—in our families, our classrooms, our workplaces. We should plant seeds of peace wherever we go. And like Johnny Appleseed, scattering seeds of peace, we can, as George Fox said, "walk cheerfully over the world," with beauty all around us.

LOVE CEREMONY

I am a big fan of ceremony. I see people come into council frazzled, tense, loud, angry. And I see how something as simple as passing around the burning sage suddenly creates an island of peace. Adolescents shyly take out their favorite poems to read during the opening ceremony, and I see the circle slowly cohere as they recognize their own souls in the poems of others. Two angry people become calm when they are able to pass a stick back and forth.

Ceremony is an ordering principle. Introduce ceremony into your life. Set aside a time to sit quietly before your altar.

Take a moment before eating to be grateful for life. Pass your invisible talking stick to a loved one, a stranger on the bus, a tree, and listen to their amazing stories. Create small islands of sacred time and space in your day. These islands will grow larger by themselves.

Peacemakers can help create ceremonies for all aspects of peacemaking. For example, when reconciliation has occurred, when a broken relationship has been healed, the occasion can be marked by a ceremony as simple as adding a stone to a stone pile near the peace table, or as elaborate as a celebration circle, in which all the participants can speak about the effect of the reconciliation on their own lives.

There are two aspects to such a ceremony—putting the conflict into the past and beginning a new future of reconciliation. My friend and teacher Sparrow Hart, a facilitator of wilderness vision quests, calls these aspects *putting away* and *taking on*. Almost every ceremony combines these two aspects—putting aside being single and going forward into married life; leaving childhood behind and becoming an adult; saying farewell to someone who has died and moving on with life.

Such ceremonies may include symbolic ways of putting away the past. The ceremony may take a symbol of the past—a photograph, an object, a stone, words written on a piece of paper—and burn or bury or break it; throw it off a cliff, or into the water, or into the wind. On one vision quest, I wrote the words *anger, arrogance,* and *ego* on three rocks and threw them into the Gila River. Other ways of putting away include washing your body, cutting your hair, sweating in a sweat lodge.

In the same way, ceremonies can symbolize taking on the new by feasting, putting on new or different clothing, changing your appearance, acquiring a new powerful object, entering into and then emerging from the water or a cave or a circle.

Even just entering into a council circle, even with one other person, even with a brief *Hey, let's circle up on this,* is a complete ceremony. Entering the sacred space and time means *taking on* the intention to listen devoutly and speak honestly, and *putting away* hierarchy, ego, fear, and self-importance. Psychologist and wilderness guide Bill Plotkin says that ceremony is a way of *saying yes to your soul.*

BE A CLOWN FOR PEACE

Here is one of my favorite stories, which comes from the Talmud. There was once a rabbi named Baruqa, who liked to visit the marketplace. One day in the market he saw, to his amazement, the prophet Elijah. He hurried over to the prophet and asked, "Of all these people, who will have a share in the World-to-Come?" Elijah shook his head sadly and said, "None." Later, two men came into the marketplace, and Rabbi Baruqa asked them who they were and what they did. They replied, "We are clowns. When people are sad, we cheer them up. When we see two people in conflict, we help them make peace." And Elijah said to Rabbi Baruqa, "Those two will have a share in the World-to-Come."

I often tell this story in my classes and seminars. And I end with a question: *Are you willing to be a clown for peace?* Are you willing to give up ego, hierarchy, power, dignity, self-importance, moral superiority? Are you willing to give up control and hand yourself over to the process? Are you willing to laugh at your imperfections?

To be a clown is to demonstrate humility. As you would expect, humility has a bad reputation in our society. But I think that the true meaning of humility is simply not to take ourselves so damn seriously. To be humble means being content with both our gifts and our limitations, not regarding others as competitors but as fellow travelers on the path. It means wasting no time in envy of others who have different gifts. It means never to be ashamed, never to need to inflate our importance in the eyes of others, never to need to buttress our self-esteem.

Humility means taking joy in the exercise of the gifts we have, rather than despairing over those we lack. Indeed, these are the very gifts we discover in the council circle that is our life. Humility means being fundamentally happy with ourselves. That is the kind of human person the spirits of the circle want us to be.

WALK IN BEAUTY EVERY DAY

If we create small islands of sacred space and time in our day, these small islands will tend to get larger. This is not inevitable; we all fail, sometimes, to live up to our best selves. But the process miraculously continues. Think what it would be like to live *always* in sacred space and time, with every person we meet—friends, relatives, strangers, animals, trees, rocks.

One of the most remarkable effects of being a peacemaker is that *fear diminishes*. The reason for this, I think, is that the things we most fear being taken from us—our status, our authority, our ego, our self-control, our importance—*we have already abandoned.* No one can take what we have already given away. Then the things we most fear—the contempt, censure, harsh light of scrutiny, the judgment that Audre Lorde describes—have no power over us. When we find ourselves in apparent conflict, we do not become decentered and confused, and we do not create narratives of victimization. We seek to meet our mutual unmet needs, and we walk cheerfully over the world, surrounded by beauty.

19
Setting Out on the Peace Path

SETTING THE INTENTION

Think about the sacrifices and rewards of being a peace-maker. Do you want to walk the peace path? Then it is time to set out.

There are several models we can use to think about this path. I would like to propose that we think about it as a *heroic journey*. On the heroic journey, the hero ventures forth from the ordinary world into sacred space and time—the magical forest—to win a gift. On the way, the hero meets adversaries, human and demonic, and allies of all sorts—animals, spirits, humans. There are sacrifices to be made, obstacles to be overcome, and finally the gift to be brought back for the good of the people.

My friend and teacher Sparrow Hart asks those who want to participate in his wilderness vision quests to see themselves as undertaking just such a heroic journey, and he asks them to answer a series of questions about how they view the journey they will soon begin. In the same way, you might want to start your own heroic journey of peacemaking by writing a letter to yourself, your spirit, your Inner Peacemaker, your best self, stating how you will bring peacemaking into your life, answering a series of questions like those Sparrow asks his participants. The letter might include the following.

Why am I called to be a peacemaker? Why do I want to be a peacemaker *now,* at this particular time? Where am I in my life right now? What is new? What has changed?

What will I leave behind? What parts of my life –status, ego, control, dignity, self-importance, moral superiority—will I leave behind in order to be a peacemaker? Do I have regrets about this? What will I need to do to cast these things aside?

What obstacles do I face? What are the obstacles that block my being a peacemaker? What is keeping me from my goals? What keeps me from taking on new things? What prevents me from letting go of that which no longer serves me? What strengths do I have to overcome these obstacles?

Who are my adversaries? What demons and ogres do I encounter? What do I fear? What do I resist? What are the attachments in my life and how do they control me? What weapons can I bring with me to face my adversaries?

Who are my allies? Who helps me be a peacemaker? What are the sources of my strength? What spirit or power do I answer to? What tools do I have to call on this power?

What is the gift I seek to bring to my people? What do I wish to call into my life? What gifts do I wish to offer to my people? What new tasks call me? How will these gifts change the way I live my life?

You might find it helpful to put the letter away, and read it in six months, to see how you have progressed on your journey.

BEGINNINGS

Walking the peace path is a journey, and the journey can begin with some small steps. Start a weekly family council circle, with a family talking stick; it may be awkward at first, and not much may happen, but remember that the family is *learning how to sit in circle together.* The day will come when a real issue presents itself, and the circle will be ready for you.

Start a small circle with some coworkers—the ones you already spend time with or eat lunch with. Meet after work, or during lunch, and pass the talking stick around. The circle does not have to be obvious; you can use a small and unobtrusive item as your stick. If others are curious, invite them to sit with you. Perhaps the circle can expand; perhaps someone will suggest using council at weekly staff meetings.

Bring a talking stick to your next parent-teacher meeting, and use it, even if you feel awkward. Ask the school principal to try setting up a council circle in just one middle school classroom. See how it works, and let it spread. Try handing your invisible talking stick to family members, friends, coworkers; take a chance, and hand it to a stranger. Hand it to a tree along the highway; hand it to the sun. Wherever you go, feel that invisible stick in your pocket. Take it out from time to time just to look at it, then put it back.

Remember that you are not just a peacemaker; you are a *carrier of council*. There will be disappointments. People in authority will be skeptical or will not want to relinquish their power and control. Institutions that claim to be doing council will simply impose the same old hierarchical, punitive, and transactional cultural values on a new model. Circle participants will be uncomfortable without the kind of structure and apparent efficiency they are used to. But your aim as a peacemaker is simply to plant seeds, some of which will grow in astonishing ways. And along the way, everywhere you go, you will hear the most wonderful stories.

You will also, from time to time, fail, because you are a human being and are fallible, and because of your lifelong hierarchical, punitive, and transactional conditioning. You will get angry and enjoy it; you will get bored and distracted and dismissive at the stories you are told: you will withhold your heart because of fear or shame. All of this is part of the path. Hand your invisible talking stick to your own best self; visit your Inner Peacemaker in the magical forest. Tell your best self honestly of your failures and frustrations, and listen devoutly to what it says in return.

And slowly, very slowly, perhaps even without being aware of it, you will find yourself changing. Your anger and fear will diminish; you will find unimagined sources of courage and determination. As you listen devoutly with your heart, you will find your heart slowly becoming, as St. Francis said, transformed and undefended. As you speak honestly from your heart, you will find, deep in yourself, the warrior virtues of transparency, vulnerability, courage, and accountability. You are in the process of disarming yourself, becoming filled with the beauty that is all around you.

APPENDIX A

Council Variations

THE WEB FORMAT

In the web format—sometimes called the *popcorn format*—the talking stick is placed in the center of the circle, rather than passed around. Any participant can pick up the stick, carry it to where he or she sits, speak, and return the stick to the center of the circle. It is called a web because the talking stick moves back and forth across the circle like a web being spun; it is called the popcorn format because participants pop up seemingly at random to take the talking stick from the center.

This format is particularly useful at the end of a council session: it allows people to tie up loose ends, summarize the proceedings, make a final contribution, or perhaps even speak for the first time after having been silent on previous rounds. Sometimes, too, a web format allows greater integration of contributions: a story can be gathered more coherently from several tellers, or participants may be able to respond more directly to someone who has just spoken.

I have found that often the stick goes around the circle

several times, and eventually people have said what they have to say—the *easy* things, the surface things. The stick is then passed around in silence, as each person hopes that someone else will open the door to the hard work, the deeper feelings, the unstated needs. Putting the stick in the center is a way of signaling that the next round has begun, and it is at this point that people may begin to struggle with the real issues.

You may have to wait a while before someone picks up the stick. Waiting requires patience and trust in the process. Waiting requires that everyone listen devoutly to the silence, awaiting the call to speak from the heart.

In my experience, someone *always* picks up the stick. In fact, once the door is open, it may be the case that a *lot* of people want to pick up the stick. When that happens, you— or someone—may say: *It looks like a lot of people want to speak. Should we start passing the stick around the circle again?*

I was once asked to participate in a circle containing ten angry parents and one very stressed school principal. The parents knew something about council, since council circles were held regularly among the children at the school. And the parents wanted no part of it. They wanted to yell, and they wanted to yell whenever they felt like it. When I first suggested passing the stick around, one parent threw the stick on the floor. Several parents had harsh words for me personally. So I suggested—just so that two people would not be yelling at once—that we put the stick in the center and that people pick it up when they had something to say. At first there was chaos. People would scramble for the stick; people would bang heads in the middle of the circle; people would try to grab the stick out of each other's hands.

Slowly, people realized that no one was communicating this way. They spontaneously began taking turns at taking the stick from the center of the circle. When someone holding the stick was interrupted, the one with the stick would say: *Excuse me, I have the stick.* People started to like the idea that they were interrupted less and less often. Things were getting calmer. I had been entirely silent this whole time. Finally, I said: *Maybe it would be easier if we passed the stick around, so that people won't have to jump up so often.* They started passing the stick. Many tensions remained at the end of the council session, but nobody had left, and people were talking with each other.

A variation on this is to give the speaker the option of either putting the stick back into the center of the circle or *passing it to another participant.* This is probably best limited to an ongoing council whose members know each other well, so that the recipient of the stick does not feel ambushed. It definitely enhances the practice of spontaneity, although, of course, the recipient, as always, has the option of silently returning the talking stick to the center, or passing it to someone else.

Another variation that I have seen is to start a council session by putting the stick in the center, waiting for someone to pick it up and begin, and then continue by passing it around the circle to the left.

THE SPIRAL FORMAT

Large groups can sometimes be unwieldy. Picture a circle of twenty participants. If everyone talks for just one minute, it has already taken twenty minutes to pass the stick around just one time. If there are forty participants, the time doubles. In some circumstances, this may turn out to be no problem at all. I once circled up with *sixty* inner-city high school girls, arranged in three irregular concentric circles. All we did for two hours was pass the stick and call in the teachers—grandmothers, mentors, absent fathers, friends who had stuck with them in hard times. It was one of the most deeply moving circles I have ever been in.

A variation suited to large circles is called the *spiral format*. Those who are ready to speak sit in a circle at the center with the others seated as witnesses in a concentric circle around them. As each participant in the inner circle finishes, he or she waits to listen to the next person, then leaves the inner circle, and a person in the outer circle moves in to sit in the empty seat and await his or her turn to speak. Waiting until the next person has finished speaking avoids the appearance of the earlier speaker quickly stepping away from the circle as if speaking were more important than listening. In this way, new speakers keep spiraling into the council from among the witnesses outside, and speakers leave their seats to become witnesses. Depending on the size of the group and the time available, it can be decided whether participants will be able to spiral in and speak more than once.

THE FISHBOWL FORMAT

The fishbowl format, like the spiral format, is useful for a group too large for universal participation, but here there is no spiraling in and out. There is a council circle in the center, and then a larger outer circle around the inner circle. The only speakers are those in the inner circle; people in the outer circle are *witnesses*. This format may also be called a *wisdom council* or a *council of elders*, where the council speakers are respected elders, or are elected representatives, or have special experience or expertise in the area being discussed. After a wilderness vision quest, there may be a council of elders held in the fishbowl format, where those returning from the hill tell their stories, one by one, in the circle of vision-quest guides, who then mirror and elaborate on the experience.

Witnesses in the fishbowl format sit around the outside of the council circle and observe the proceedings. One purpose for having witnesses is for them to understand and eventually comment on the *process* of the council, and not the content of anything said. When witnesses speak in council about the council, they observe the four intentions, with the purpose of improving the council process.

Another purpose is for witnesses just to hear the complete stories—the understandings, feelings, needs, fears, regrets—of the circle participants, especially as those stories relate to the witnesses themselves. In one high school, boys and girls had held separate council circles for some time and had become comfortable with the process. Then, on one occasion, the boys were invited to be witnesses to the girls' council, in which the girls spoke openheartedly about their fears of sexual violence; and on another occasion, the girls were invited to be witnesses at the boys' council, in which the boys spoke openheartedly about their fears of rejection and humiliation by the girls.

At a conference on black-and-brown unity, Hispanic participants were invited to be witnesses to a circle in which

African American participants talked about their experiences with Hispanics. The witnesses were shocked as they heard, to their amazement, the black speakers express both stereotypes and anger about Hispanics: *They make good gardeners. They are stealing our jobs.* After the council session, several Hispanic witnesses sought out the African American participants, challenged them on what they had said, and invited them to circle up together. And at that circle, based on what was said earlier, the real healing work began.

THE DYADIC FORMAT

The dyadic format is a special case of the fishbowl format that is particularly useful for healing disputes or tensions between two members of the group. In this format, the only council speakers are the two persons, and the rest of the group function as witnesses and supporters not of either participant in the central circle but of the process itself. The silent supportive presence of the witnesses can help the two participants to keep to the four intentions as they pass the talking stick back and forth; the witnesses may provide an affirmative *aho!* after each of the two participants speaks. Even more, each of the two participants may request the presence of a supporter, who does nothing but stand behind the participant silently with a hand on the participant's shoulder.

Warm-ups

GAMES

Games and council go together, because they both build trust and therefore help to build cohesion in groups and communities. People in council often meet as strangers. One of the most important factors that turns a group of strangers into a community is learning that they can reveal themselves without penalty. Through games they learn that they can be foolish and still esteemed. This knowledge gives them the courage to take the risk of telling complete stories. My wife calls games *council foreplay*.

Learning to Be Foolish

For many of these activities, the goal is to break down barriers by allowing—even encouraging—participants to behave foolishly. Being granted permission to behave in a silly manner at the outset can be quite liberating; the prospect of looking foolish in the future is less intimidating if the participant has behaved foolishly already without adverse consequence.

But there is a deeper meaning to foolishness. To be a peacemaker—to sit in circle with others—is to give up ego, give up being right, give up hierarchy, and be, as I said earlier, a clown for peace. Indeed, there are games whose *only* purpose is to allow people to be foolish. In one such game, the participants sit in a circle and a number of small objects are passed out, evenly spaced around the circle. Each person with an object can pass it to the person immediately to the right or left; a person who receives an object can also pass it in either direction. If a participant finds two objects in his or her lap, the player must make a loud awful noise, and then pass the two objects in opposite directions. The faster the game, the more people get caught; the more people who get caught, the more loud awful noises there are.

Here is a game that combines foolishness with participants learning each other's names. The participants stand in a circle. One participant says his or her name and accompanies that name with a gesture or posture or action such as clapping hands, waving arms, jumping up and down, turning in a circle—the more creative the better. The group then repeats both the name and the action. Then the next participant does the same, and this time the group repeats the name and gesture of the second person followed by the name and gesture of the first person. By the time several participants have given their names, the group is saying the names and gesturing, jumping, and spinning. Mistakes by individuals are inevitable and add to the enjoyment. By the end of the circle everyone will know everyone else's name, and everyone will have behaved with socially acceptable foolishness.

Learning about Each Other

A number of these activities are known as *icebreakers*. The goal of such activities is to get participants to learn something about each other, celebrate the diversity of the group, and identify group members with common interests or experiences.

For example, each participant can find a partner and discover something they have in common that is not visible. This can range from the simple to the complex, from both of them having tattoos or riding motorcycles or being vegetarians to both having rappelled off an overpass on a major interstate highway. Then the group gathers again and, for each pair, uses a twenty-questions-type format to try to guess what the pair's commonality is. Wrong guesses can be as much fun as correct ones.

A variation can be a human treasure hunt. Each participant is given a list and must find a participant who fits each description on the list—for example, someone who has gotten lost for more than three hours or has been in a parade or has held public office or has a twin. Each human treasure can be listed only once.

One of my favorite icebreakers is called *two truths and a lie*. The participants, one at a time, each state three facts about themselves to the group; two of the facts are true, and one is false. Some versions of this game elaborate facts into stories. The group may ask the speaker questions for a specified period, usually a few minutes, to explore the claims being made. Then the group votes, and the speaker reveals the truth. Once the truth has been revealed, part of the enjoyment is then for the group to ask additional questions.

I have played the game with people who have turned out to be world travelers, Olympic swimmers, and presidential bodyguards.

Here is a variation, especially for people who know each other, or think they know each other. On small cards, all the participants write something true about themselves that no one else in the group knows, for example: *My grandmother was a professional trombone player; I have a tattoo of a rose on my butt; I once drank fondue through a straw.* Then the cards are read out loud, either one right after the other or spaced throughout the session, and for each statement the participants guess who wrote it. Here again, wrong guesses, revealing participants' preconceptions about each other, can be as revealing—and as much fun—as correct ones.

A game can begin as an icebreaker and evolve into something deeper and more metaphorical. In the game *Who here . . .?* participants stand in a circle and a brief question, beginning with the words *Who here . . .* is read. These questions begin simply: for example, *Who here is an oldest child? Who here grew up in the suburbs? Who here was raised by a single parent?*

As each question is read, each person who can answer the question affirmatively crosses the circle to the other side. Participants may choose to pass on any question and not cross the circle, even if they think the description applies to them.

Then the questions start probing issues of self-identity. For example: *Who here is white? Who here is a person of color? Who here is Muslim? Who here is a single parent? Who here has ever been homeless? Who here was held back a grade in school? Who here does not speak English as their first language?*

This can be a very moving exercise, as people wrestle with the limits of their comfort in self-disclosure. I have seen the group break into spontaneous applause when a member first hesitates, then decides, and then courageously crosses the circle to the other side. It can be moving, too, when people discover, often to their amazement, that others in the group share their background and troubles—has been in prison, has received public assistance, comes from a family where substance abuse or violence was a problem. What is most striking and revelatory, especially in the context of a circle addressing conflict and violence, is when, in response to the question *Who here has ever harmed another person?* everyone in the group simultaneously crosses the circle together.

Learning to Speak

Storytelling games are a way to get people comfortable with speaking in front of others in the council circle. Some people are gifted natural storytellers, but even the less articulate can be encouraged to participate. Round-robin stories are useful for getting everyone involved and can, in fact, be very funny. The first person is handed the talking stick, given the opening line *Once upon a time . . .* and then has one minute to tell part of the story. At the end of the minute, the stick is passed to the next person, who must continue the story. Part of the fun is to end your turn with some totally unexpected story development, to which the next person must quickly adjust. This is a good way for people to learn to listen devoutly, without preparing a mental script, and then speak spontaneously.

One way of encouraging participation, even by the inarticulate, is to pass around prepared cards containing words or pictures to all the participants. A card might have the word *tree* or *chipmunk* or *Bozo the clown* written on it. I have seen people use tarot cards for the same purpose. No one knows what is on anyone else's cards. As it becomes each person's turn, that person must weave the word or picture on the card into the story, the more humorously the better—for example, *And then the hero climbed a tree; The evil magician turned the princess into a talking chipmunk; And who should appear but—Bozo the clown!* Elaboration should be encouraged, but even the most taciturn or shy group member can come up with a sentence about a tree, and the contribution should be applauded.

Games can be intensely serious. I once had the privilege of attending a week-long training on protracted interethnic conflict by Mennonite peacemaker John Paul Lederach. He told us of a time he was working with government leaders in a country striving to make the transition from military to democratic rule. There were many conflicts and apparent impasses. He assigned these participants to groups of five, mixing military and civilian leaders, and he told them that each group should collectively compose a letter to their grandchildren, titled *How I Helped Bring Peace to Our Country.*

DRUMMING

Father Dave Kelly of the Precious Blood Ministry of Reconciliation in Chicago leads incarcerated youth at the Cook County Juvenile Temporary Detention Center in drumming circles. After they drum together, they stay in circle and talk. These tough kids, many of them gang members, talk about their lives, their hopes, and, remarkably, about their fears. Father Dave knows that drumming in a circle opens doors, creates cohesion, and builds community in astonishing ways.

Everyone enjoys drumming; humans have probably been drumming for hundreds of thousands of years. People will—when they think no one is looking—drum on the steering wheels of their cars, on the desktops in their offices, and on their own bodies.

Drumming can help the group create cohesion in several ways. First, as we have discussed, taking the risk of appearing foolish in front of others, without in fact being penalized, helps to build trust and confidence in the group. Second, drumming, just by itself, creates group interactions that serve as metaphors—implicit or explicit—for forms of cohesiveness that can then be carried into the council circle.

Drum Circles

There are two types of group drumming that can be used as part of a council circle, which we can call *drum circle* and *trance drumming*. In a drum circle, everyone does something different, and ideally, the different thing each person does creates a single perfect whole. Drumming in a drum circle can require intense concentration, to keep track of the fundamental beat, called the *one,* which can get buried in layers of sound.

More important, it requires thoughtful consideration of just what the evolving rhythmic structure requires, *at that moment,* to be more complete. For example, a participant may perfect the rhythm with, say, a single shake of a rattle on the seventh of eight beats. The smallest of contributions may be just what is necessary to make the rhythm complete. Since the totality shifts as participants move in and out or change their contribution, what is required from each participant changes from moment to moment.

To abandon ego in a drum circle, to trust in the drum *process,* requires each participant to act both spontaneously and leanly, so that—just as in council—the almost autonomous web of connections among the drums can lead the process toward an unforeseen perfection. A successful drum circle is exhilarating, miraculous.

Trance Drumming

In trance drumming, on the other hand, everyone does the *same* thing. The rhythm is repetitive, although it may be complex and is frequently rapid. For example, a typical trance-drum rhythm is the eight-beat sequence **one**-two-three **one**-two-three **one**-two, where the boldface type indicates an emphasized beat. A more complex rhythm is the sixteen-beat sequence **one**-two-three **one**-two-three **one**-two-three **one**-two **one**-two.

The complexity and rapidity are important. It is not difficult—in fact, it is boring—for the whole group just to drum **one**-two-three-four over and over again in unison; where the rhythm is, say, **one**-two-three **one**-two-three **one**-two, however, it can require concentration and effort to get everyone doing the same thing at the same time. Some group members will pick up the rhythm quickly, and some will require encouragement; yet even the most agile learner can lose the beat and have to stop drumming and listen carefully—perhaps even to one of the slower learners—to pick it up again. As with drum circles, to keep a trance rhythm going for ten or more minutes can be an exhilarating experience of group interaction and cohesion.

"Moe Sits in Council"

The following is a chapter from a novel in progress, titled The White-Haired Man. *The protagonist, Moe, is a police detective in an inner-city neighborhood that is filled with apathy and violence. In this excerpt, he is introduced to a council circle for the first time. It is a distillation of many circles in which I have participated. The chapter is, of course, a quite abbreviated version of a process that can take a much longer time, but I hope it gives some of the flavor of this sort of circle.*

Moe saw that they were standing in front of a storefront church. On the window someone had painted Church of the Redeeming Rock of Zion and, beneath that, Reverend William Nudge.

"You will go inside and join a meeting," the white-haired man said in his usual precise and unaccented English. "As you participate, Detective, please remember that for everyone there you are the voice of the community."

The white-haired man turned and walked away. Moe had no idea what he was talking about. Left alone in the tiny entryway, Moe turned the knob on the door, which opened, and he walked inside.

The first thing Moe saw were rows of folding chairs lined up to face a lectern and a large golden cross hanging on the opposite wall. Standing among the chairs was a tall black man, his hair cropped short, wearing an immaculate pearl-gray suit and a matching shirt with a clerical collar. The man rushed forward and shook Moe's hand, saying, "Thank you so much for coming, Detective. Your presence here means a lot to everyone. Please follow me."

The pastor led Moe to a doorway, which opened onto a steep flight of narrow stairs leading downward. "Please," the pastor said, gesturing, so Moe descended the stairs carefully, since there was no handrail, and found himself in the basement, followed closely by the pastor.

The basement looked like many storefront church basements Moe had seen before—gray speckled linoleum tiles on the floor, thin wood-patterned paneling warping on the walls, some opened cardboard boxes full of hymnals, a dusty glass-fronted bookcase filled with leaning rows of old books. Four people were sitting in gray metal folding chairs that had been set in a circle in the middle of the floor. The fifth chair was empty.

These storefront churches came and went in the precinct, Moe knew. They served primarily the black population, although increasing numbers of younger Hispanics found the evangelical fervor of their services attractive. They formed quickly around individual charismatic preachers, many of whom had little theological training and no strong denominational ties, and they often disappeared when their leader, for one reason or another, moved on.

It had been in a thousand church basements like this that the civil rights movement had taken its shape and direction. These little churches were the bedrock of the black community—gathering places, sources of gossip, solace for the grieving, and support in times of trouble.

The pastor turned at the bottom of the stairs. "I will leave you here," he said. "I wish you God's blessing on this work." The pastor walked back up the steep steps, leaving Moe facing the people sitting in the circle of chairs.

Moe realized that one of the chairs was occupied by Tomas Ramirez, the man who ran the bodega where Moe bought his coffee and cookies, and who had given the speech at the precinct captain's monthly meeting.

To Tomas's left sat one of the skinniest women Moe had ever seen. She appeared to be at least eighty years old, and she sat upright on the rickety chair, her feet flat on the floor and knees together, her bony frame and wrinkled coal-black skin covered in a polka-dotted dress that fell over her knees to the middle of her calves. Her right arm was in a blue canvas sling. Moe recognized her from the precinct. She was Maman Françoise, the baker of cookies.

To the left of Maman Françoise sat a heavy-set black woman wearing a generic light-blue waitress uniform made of a polyester crepe that sat uneasily on her thick body. She wore the heavy sensible flat-heeled shoes of a woman who stood on her feet for many hours at a time. On her uniform there was a white plastic name tag that said *Michelle*.

In the next chair was a nervous-looking black kid, high school age, hair cropped short. Something about the way the kid sat made Moe think he was related to the waitress, probably her son. Moe had seen a lot of kids who sat like this, trying not to show that they were worried. *Here is a good-looking kid,* Moe thought, *who looks like he is in a whole lot of trouble.*

The chair to the left of the boy was empty. Tomas gestured toward the empty seat. Moe sat down in it, with no idea what he was supposed to be doing.

As soon as Moe sat, Tomas turned to him and said, "Thank you for joining us here today, Detective. We have all had some individual preparation for what we will do here today, but you and I did not have a chance to meet together. I am sure you will catch on quickly. What we do here today is a very human thing."

Tomas faced the group. "You remember how this works," he said. "We sit in a circle, and we pass around this talking stick." He held up a stick that someone had decorated with strips of cloth, some beads, a few feathers. "Whoever holds the talking stick gets to speak, and everybody else listens."

He waited until he saw nods from the participants. "There will be no interruptions, no questions, no *desafío*"— he hesitated, searching for the word—"no challenges, no comments. We will speak one at a time, honestly from our hearts, and we will listen devoutly with our hearts to each person who speaks. We are agreed about this?"

Tomas paused as people nodded. Moe wasn't sure he agreed with any of it, but he decided to wait and see what happened.

"We are not here to punish Denton," Tomas said, nodding at the teenage boy sitting in the circle. "We are not here to judge him. Denton has harmed another member of the community, and he has agreed to come here to try to make it right. Maman Françoise has agreed not to bring this matter to the police if we can get it resolved here. She can change her mind at any time. Denton knows that this is, for him, an alternative to the juvenile justice system."

The fuck it is, Moe thought, but he kept silent as Tomas passed the stick to the skinny black woman on his left.

The woman took the stick awkwardly with her left hand and held it close to her narrow chest. "My name is Armentine Credeur Françoise," she said, "but here dey call me Maman Françoise. I have had tree husban in my life an twelve chillen, eight a dem still alive. I have twenny-two granchillen, and for dem I bake cookies and cakes and send them far away to where they live now. Now I get de social security and I sell cookies to Mistah Ramirez here. Dat is how I live.

"But you," she said, pointing with the stick in her left hand at the black high school kid, "you took dis away. I comin back from de bank where I cash de check an you grab my purse. You grab so hard you dislocate my shoulder. You take my purse and you push me down. I am on de groun and you runnin, you, an you laughin at how you hurt dis ol lady. You should be ashame, you.

"You take my money, you. *Co faire?* What you spen dat on? What so important dat you push me on de groun? But you worse than that, you. You don jus take my money. You take away my job, because I can bake no more wit dis shoulder broke. And you make me fraid to go out, now. You take away my soul partwise when you hurt my shoulder, when you push me on de groun. I been hurt before in dis life, but now, in dis circle, I no take no more.

"You *dépouille*, you. You a mess. What you do wit you life? You be tief all time? Now I tell you what I feel here, what you gone do make dis right?"

Her gaze was fierce, directed right at Denton. Maman Françoise had pain and fury in her eyes, and grief for what had been taken from her, and an unyielding determination to see it made right. Denton looked back at her and lowered his eyes. Maman Françoise passed the stick to the woman in the waitress uniform.

"You, boy," the woman said, turning to her left to face her son. "I am ashamed and embarrassed here today. I don't want to feel that way. I want to be proud of you, and maybe someday I will. But right here and right now, you have to face up to what you did.

"Miss Françoise, I do want to apologize to you on behalf of my son. What he did to you was wrong in so many ways that I don't even know where to begin. I can only tell you that this was not how he was raised. I tried to raise him to be a good boy. I would like to be able to blame the gangs, but I can't. He made his own decisions. Maybe I'm at fault too. I don't know. I did my best to raise him up right. But I can assure you that he will be accountable for what he has done. I will make no excuses.

"I am glad we are here in this house of God, so that we can do our best to keep this boy out of the system. I know he will pretend that he doesn't care, but I know he does. I can only pray to God, here in his house, that my boy learns from this. I will stand behind whatever you all decide." She put the stick in her left hand and passed it, backhanded, and not gently, to her son.

The boy was trying to look tough, but Moe could see tears in his eyes. "Look, I'm sorry," he said to the fierce woman staring at him. "I didn't know you, not as a person, really. I figured I'd get some money, buy myself something nice, cause my momma works all the time, and she never seems to get ahead at all." He looked at his mother, and then looked away. "I let you down, momma. It was stupid. Look, Maman Françoise, I didn't know you. I'm sorry I hurt you. I was stupid." He looked at his mother again. "And I was mean. I apologize to you. I'm sorry. Please don't let them send me away." He held the stick for what seemed like a long time. He opened his mouth twice more to speak, but each time he said nothing, and then he passed the stick to Moe.

Moe held the stick in his hand. It was warm from the hands of the three others who had spoken before him. He did not know what to say. He thought this kid ought to be in juvenile detention. He felt profoundly uncomfortable bypassing the system, letting this kid get away with what he had done. All that was going on here, he thought, was just words that the kid would soon forget.

"I have been a police detective for a lot of years," he said. He spoke directly to the kid, looking him in the eye. "I think there is something you need to know. This is not just a private quarrel between you and Maman Françoise. Other people are involved. You have now involved your mother, the reverend upstairs, Mr. Ramirez here." Holding the stick was giving him a strange comfort in speaking.

"And it goes beyond that," he said. "You have made people just a little more afraid to leave their homes. You have helped to create mistrust in what should be a community. People will be just a little more afraid of kids, of young black kids like you, a little more reluctant to help, a little more mistrustful, a little more vengeful. People will live just a little more in fear because of what you did, because you did not think about the consequences.

"You have broken trust. You have broken the thread that binds people together. We could just ship you off to a juvenile detention someplace, but that wouldn't repair the harm you have done to Maman Françoise, to your mother, to everyone who lives here. I have seen too many kids go down this path. It's time to grow up. It's time to be accountable for what you have done."

Moe looked around to see people looking at him and nodding. He did not know what else to say. He started to pass the stick back to Tomas, but at the last moment he paused.

"There are people here who care about you," he said, "in spite of what you have done. These are all people who care what happens to you. Be mindful how you repay them." He paused, and nothing more came to him. This time he passed the stick.

Tomas took the stick and held it close to his chest. He sat there with his eyes closed. The moment stretched out, and then he opened his eyes and began to speak very softly. "I think there are those who think you should just be turned over to the system," he said, "to be sent away from your home, to be locked in a cage and punished, to be hurt and humiliated in order to pay for the hurt and humiliation you have caused to Maman Françoise. They say that would be justice. But that is the justice of the oppressor. We want to have healing. We want to have sacred justice.

"I think that the way to keep you from doing this again is not to punish you, and not to control you with the threat of punishment, but for you to become a better human being. So now the question is: How do we make that happen? How do we bring you back into the community whose trust you have broken? How can you make Maman Françoise whole again and regain our trust? That is, above all, for Maman Françoise to say." He passed the stick to his left.

Maman Françoise held the talking stick, with its ribbons and feathers, before her like a weapon.

"You will bake, you," she said, firmly.

Everyone was looking at the thin old woman in the polka-dot dress. "Yes, you, you will bake, in my kitchen. Two hour ever day, in my kitchen, to hep make de cookies and muffins for me to sell to de bodega. For four month, until dis shoulder betta, you will bake." Maman Françoise looked around the circle. "You go in de detention, you boy," she said, "dey eat you up, you learn nuttin but be tief. In my kitchen, you bake, learn sometin good, you make right de hurt you do me."

The stick passed to the boy's mother. "Thank you," she said. "That is more than fair. If he will do this, then he will be in your house, two hours every day, for four months. I will make sure of it. I will be in your debt for the rest of my days."

The boy held the stick. He was blinking his eyes rapidly. "I will bake," he said. Tears were leaking from the corners of his eyes, but he managed to smile. "Will you teach me how to make pies?"

The boy handed the stick to his left. Moe saw something new in the kid, and in Maman Françoise too—a kind of strength, a shared dignity. *Holy shit,* Moe thought. *What just happened here?* He didn't have anything to say, so he passed the stick silently to Tomas.

Index

BOOKS OF RELATED INTEREST

The Book of Ho'oponopono
The Hawaiian Practice of Forgiveness and Healing
by Luc Bodin, M.D., Nathalie Bodin Lamboy, and Jean Graciet

Remapping Your Mind
The Neuroscience of Self-Transformation through Story
by Lewis Mehl-Madrona, M.D., Ph.D.
With Barbara Mainguy, M.A.

Narrative Medicine
The Use of History and Story in the Healing Process
by Lewis Mehl-Madrona, M.D., Ph.D.

Speaking with Nature
Awakening to the Deep Wisdom of the Earth
by Sandra Ingerman and Llyn Roberts

The Cherokee Full Circle
A Practical Guide to Ceremonies and Traditions
by J. T. Garrett and Michael Tlanusta Garrett

Medicine of the Cherokee
The Way of Right Relationship
by J. T. Garrett and Michael Tlanusta Garrett

Walking on the Wind
Cherokee Teachings for Harmony and Balance
by Michael Tlanusta Garrett

The Zero Point Agreement
How to Be Who You Already Are
by Julie Tallard Johnson

INNER TRADITIONS • BEAR & COMPANY
P.O. Box 388, Rochester, VT 05767
1-800-246-8648
www.InnerTraditions.com

Or contact your local bookseller